Monday's River Dance designed and quilted by Jeanette Cameron.

D1285843

Editors: Jenifer Dick and Edie McGinnis
Production Editor: Diane McLendon
Tech Editor: Jane Miller
Designer: Kim Walsh
Photography: Aaron T. Leimkuehler
Production assistance: Jo Ann Groves
Quilt Contributors: Jeanette Cameron, Suann Cole, Wendy Dillingham, Sandra Gilreath, Charlotte O'Leary and Nancy Turtle

Published by: Kansas City Star Books
1729 Grand Blvd.
Kansas City, Missouri, USA 64108

First edition, first printing
ISBN: 978-1-935362-26-5

Library of Congress Control Number:
2009924512

Printed in the United States of America by Walsworth Publishing Co., Marceline, Missouri

To order copies, call toll-free 866-834-7467.

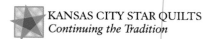
KANSAS CITY STAR QUILTS
Continuing the Tradition

The Quilter's Home Page

www.PickleDish.com
www.PickleDishStore.com

My Stars

Patterns from *The Kansas City Star* • Volume I

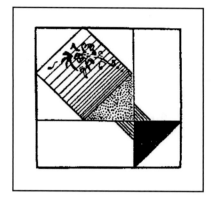
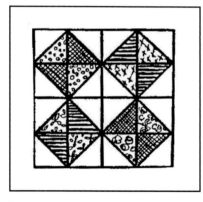
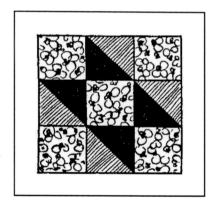
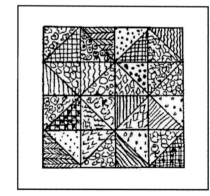
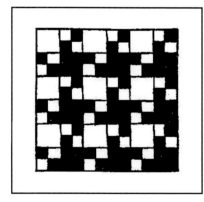

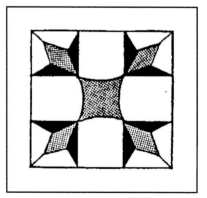

Kansas City Star Quilts would like to thank...

Edie McGinnis for her diligent work on redrafting the patterns. If it wasn't for her, My Star Collection subscribers wouldn't receive their patterns each week. She does an excellent job of choosing the patterns and reworking them to today's standards and techniques.

Jenifer Dick for her patience and organization with editing the My Star Collection patterns each week. It's a big task, and we appreciate her enthusiasm.

Kim Walsh for her attention to detail and design expertise. She lays out the patterns each week, and graciously agreed to design this book for us.

Doug Weaver for his support and confidence. When I presented him with the idea of My Star Collection, he said "Go for it!" And look where it's taken us!

Aaron Leimkuehler for his beautiful photography. He really knows how to capture the beauty of quilts.

Jane Miller for her keen eye and patience. Her ability to negotiate tight deadlines, while catching edits, is remarkable!

Jo Ann Groves for her keen eye and amazing talent. Her fine detailing of photographs makes the book a visual treat.

Our quilt friends for submitting their quilts to be published in this book.

Diane McLendon
Editor

About My Star Collection

My Star Collection is a weekly subscription service where subscribers download a pdf pattern – from *The Kansas City Star's* historical 1928-1961 collection – each week. The subscription is for a year of patterns – 52 in all! For more information or to sign up, visit subscriptions.pickledish.com.

TABLE OF CONTENTS

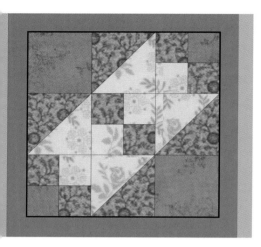

Broken Sugar Bowl

Block Size: 12" finished

Broken Sugar Bowl

Fabric Needed:

green, dark pink and pink print

Cutting Directions

From dark pink, cut

2 - 2 1/2" squares (template C)

2 - 4 1/2" squares (template A)

From pink print, cut

4 - 2 1/2" squares (template C)

2 - 4 7/8" squares

(or cut 4 triangles using template B)

From green, cut

6 - 2 1/2" squares (template C)

2 - 4 7/8" squares

(or cut 4 triangles using template B)

To Make the Block

Draw a line from corner to corner on the diagonal on the reverse side of the 4 7/8" pink print squares. Place the pink print square atop a green 4 7/8" square with right sides facing. Sew 1/4" on both sides of the drawn line. Use your rotary cutter and cut on the drawn line. Open the unit and press toward the darker fabric. This makes a half-square triangle unit. Each square will yield two half-square triangles. You need 4 for this block.

Sew a green 2 1/2" square to a dark pink 2 1/2" square. Now sew a pink print 2 1/2" square to a green 2 1/2" square. Sew the two rows together as shown, making a four-patch unit. You need to make two of these four-patch units.

You'll need to make another four-patch unit for the center of the block. Sew a green 2 1/2" square to a pink print square. Sew a pink print square to a green 2 1/2" square. Sew the two strips together to make a four-patch unit.

Sew the units into rows.
Row 1 - Sew a dark pink square to a half-square triangle. Then add a four-patch.

Row 2 - Sew a half-square triangle unit to a four-patch unit. Add another half-square triangle.

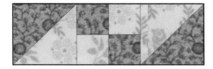

Row 3 - Sew a four-patch unit to a half-square triangle unit. End the row with a dark pink square.

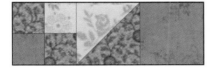

Sew the rows together to complete the block.

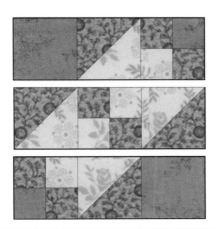

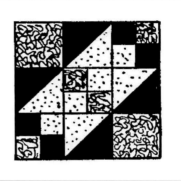

From *The Kansas City Star*,
July 22, 1942:
Number 694

This pattern was sent to The Weekly Star by Mrs. J. H. Perry, Star route 2, Williamsville, Mo. It was a favorite of her grandmother because it offered opportunity for working up odd scraps of all kinds of print. Any combination of colors may be used.

History of the Block

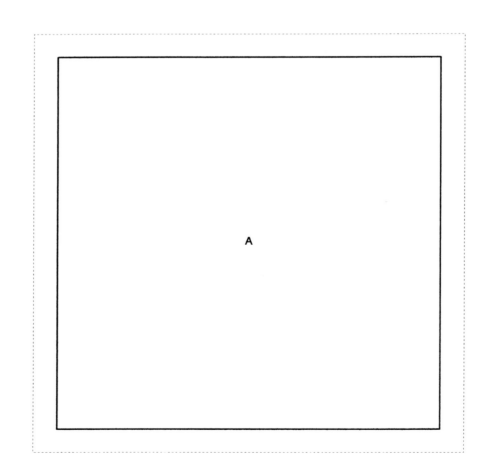

Template

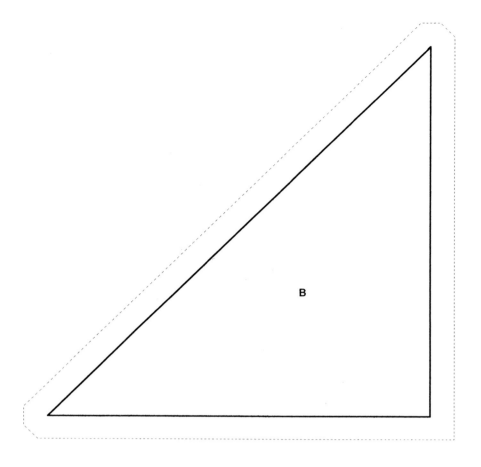

B

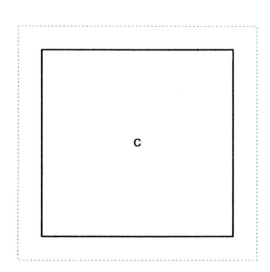

C

Template

Appeared in *The Star* **August 15, 1956**

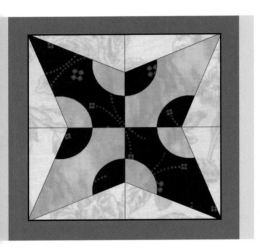

**Caps for Witches
and Dunces**

Block Size: 12" finished

Caps for Witches and Dunces

Fabric needed:

orange, brown and cream

Cutting Directions

From brown fabric, cut

2 pieces using template C

2 pieces using template D

2 pieces using template E

From orange fabric, cut

2 pieces using template C

2 pieces using template D

2 pieces using template E

From background fabric, cut

4 triangles using template A

4 triangles using template B

To Make the Block

Stitch a brown E piece to an orange C piece. Then add the brown D piece.

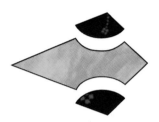

Sew the A and B triangles on next. Make two units like this.

Reverse the colors. Sew an orange E piece to a brown C piece then add the orange D piece.

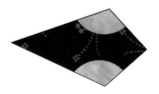

Sew the A and B triangles on next. Make two units like this.

Refer to the colored diagram and sew the four sections together to complete the block.

From *The Kansas City Star*,
August 15, 1956:
Number 990

This interesting quilt block design might be applied on a background fabric in any of the colors appearing in the figure. It is a contribution from Mrs. H. T. Christi, route 5, box 300, Magnolia, Ark.

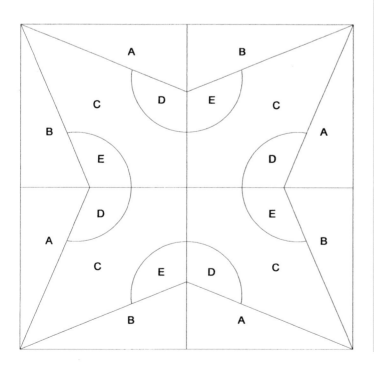

History of the Block

Caps for Witches and Dunces

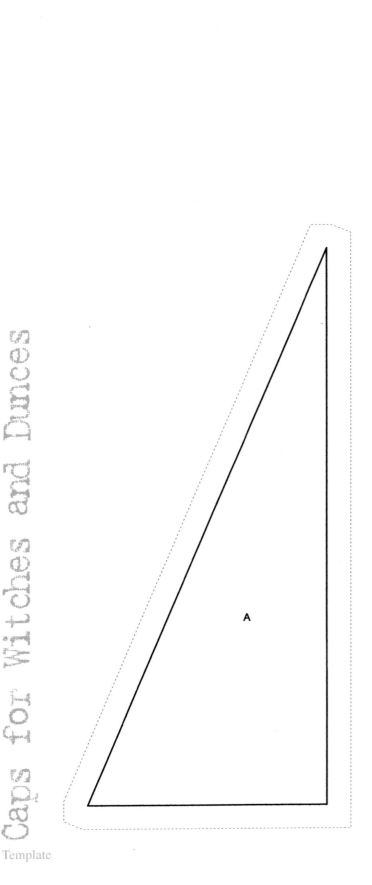

A

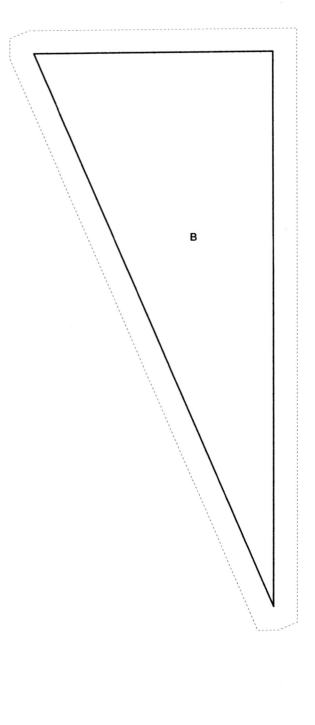

B

Template

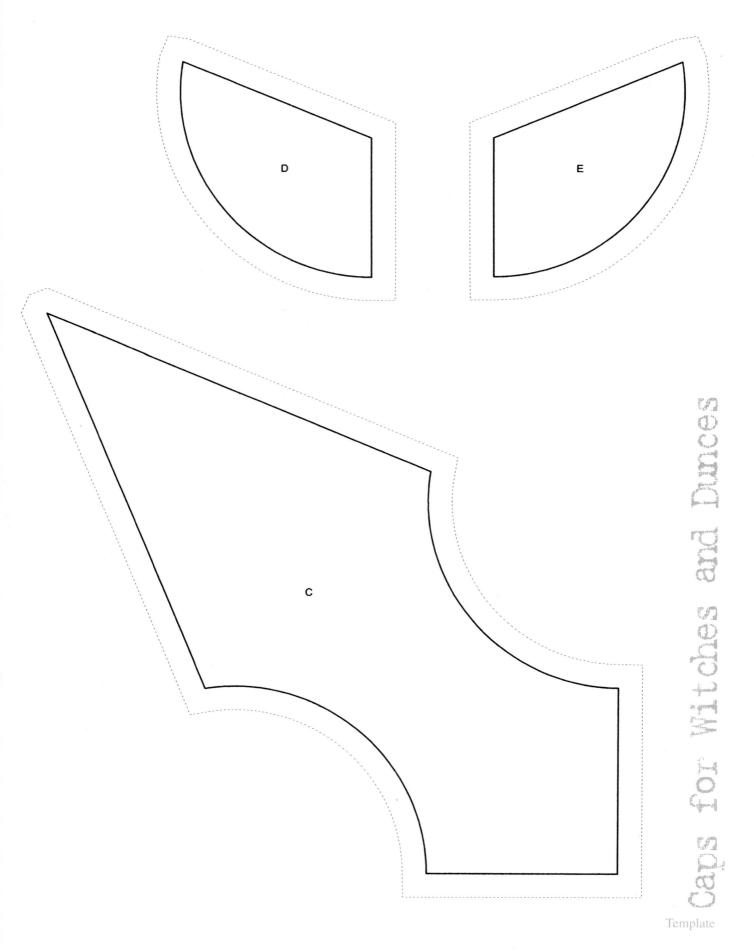

D

E

C

Caps for Witches and Dunces

Appeared in *The Star* **December 24, 1940**

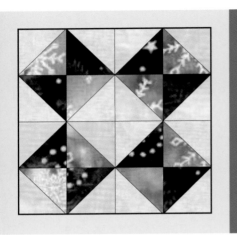

Four Patch Fox and Goose

Block Size: 12" finished

Fabric needed:
2 light backgrounds,
2 medium fabrics and 1 dark fabric.

Cutting Directions

From dark fabric, cut
4 - 3 7/8" squares
(8 triangles using template A)

From one medium fabric, cut
2 - 3 7/8" squares
(4 triangles using template A)

From one medium fabric, cut
2 - 3 7/8" squares
(4 triangles using template A)

From one light background fabric, cut
4 - 3 7/8" squares
(8 triangles using template A)

From one light background fabric, cut
4 - 3 7/8" squares
(8 triangles using template A)

To Make the Block

This block is made using half-square triangle units.

To make half-square triangles, draw a line from corner to corner on the diagonal on the reverse side of the lightest fabric. Place a light square atop a darker square and sew 1/4" on each side of the line. Use your rotary cutter and cut on the line. Open each unit and press toward the darkest fabric.

Make 4 half-square triangle units using the lightest background fabric and one of the medium fabrics.

Make 4 half-square triangle units using the lightest background fabric and the dark fabric.

Make 4 half-square triangle units using the darker background fabric and the dark fabric.

Make 4 half-square triangle units using the darker background fabric and the medium fabric.

Sew the half-square triangles together in rows of four as shown.

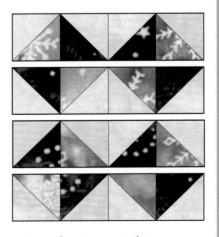

Sew the rows together to complete the block.

Four Patch Fox and Goose

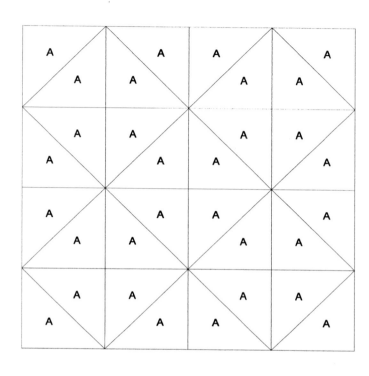

Four Patch Fox and Goose

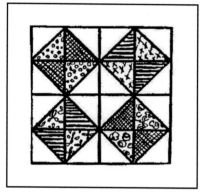

From *The Kansas City Star*,
December 24, 1940:
Number 635

Before she was old enough to go to school Mrs. Eugal Pope, Star route, Marquand, Mo., drew pictures to entertain herself. This one, which she called Four Patch Fox and Goose Board, was later made up for a quilt block pattern.

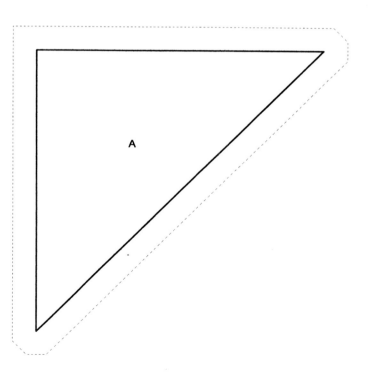

template

A

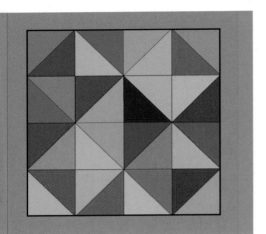

Flying Colors

Block Size: 12" finished

Flying colors is a true scrap quilt pattern. Use this as a "Stash Buster" and get rid of those small leftover fabric scraps.

Fabric needed

Scraps of all colors but must be at least a 3 7/8" square or large enough to cut triangles using the template provided.

Cutting Directions
If you use the template,

cut 32 triangles. Use dark, medium and light fabric scraps. Make half-square triangle units by sewing the triangles together along the diagonal. Open the units and press toward the darkest fabric. You need to make 16 half-square triangles.

If you are using a rotary cutter,

Cut 16 – 3 7/8" squares. Draw a line on the diagonal from corner to corner on the reverse side of the lightest colored squares. Place a light square atop a dark square and sew 1/4" on either side of the line. Use your rotary cutter and cut on the line, open each unit and press toward the darkest fabric.

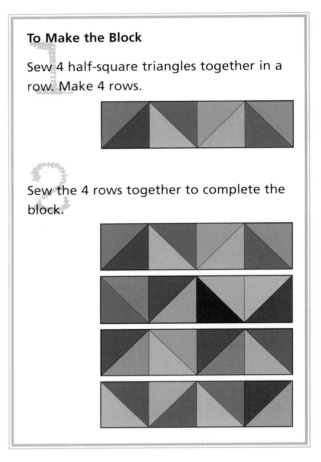

To Make the Block

Sew 4 half-square triangles together in a row. Make 4 rows.

Sew the 4 rows together to complete the block.

Flying Colors

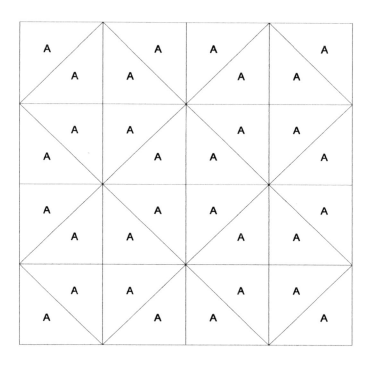

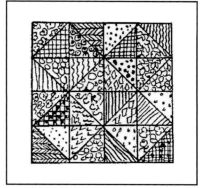

From **The Kansas City Star**, **November 5, 1958:** Number 1027

The title, Flying Colors, was given to this quilt block by Mrs. Mart Ledbetter, Witter, Ark., its designer, because she pieced it from flying bits or leftovers from other quilts.

History of the Block

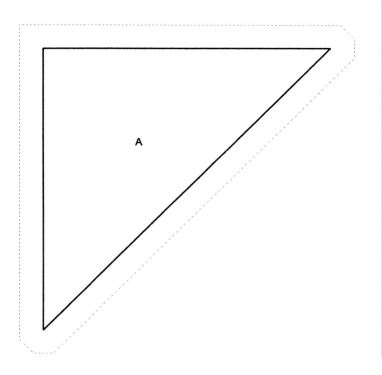

A

template

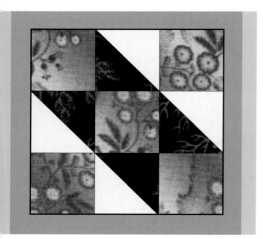

Contrary Wife

Block Size: 12" finished

Fabric needed:

dark blue, medium blue print and light blue

Cutting Directions

From dark blue, cut

2 - 4 7/8" squares

(or four triangles using template B)

From medium blue print, cut

5 - 4 1/2" squares (template A)

From light blue, cut

2 - 4 7/8" squares

(or 4 triangles using template B)

To Make the Block

Draw a line from corner to corner on the diagonal on the reverse side of the 4 7/8" light blue squares. Place the light blue square atop a dark blue 4 7/8" square with right sides facing. Sew 1/4" on both sides of the drawn line. Use your rotary cutter and cut on the drawn line. Open the unit and press toward the darker fabric. This makes a half-square triangle unit. Each square will yield two half-square triangles. You need 4 for this block.

Sew a medium blue square to a half-square triangle. Then add a medium blue square. Make two rows like this.

Sew a half-square triangle to a medium blue square. Add a half-square triangle unit. This is the center row.

Sew the rows together as shown to complete the block.

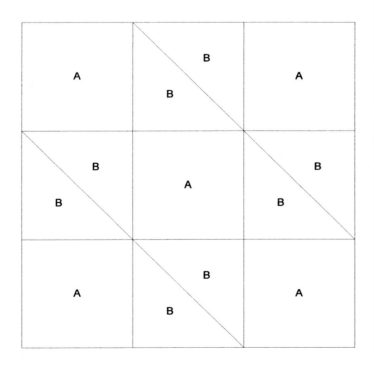

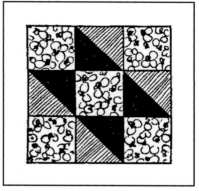

From *The Kansas City Star*,
August 27, 1941:
Number 658

"The Contrary Wife" was originated by Mrs. Bertha Oglesby, R. R. 1, Arkinda, Ark.

History of the Block

A

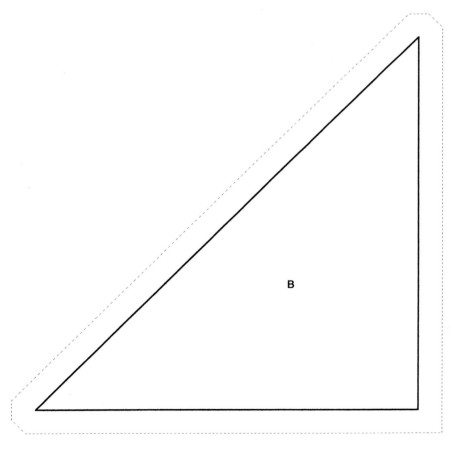

B

Contrary Wife

Template

Garden Party by Charlotte O'Leary. Quilted by Heirloom Quilting Studio, David & SueAnn Suderman.

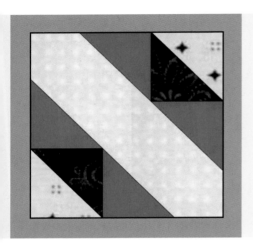

Friendship
Name Chain

Block size: 6" finished

Fabric needed:

red, black print, black and white shirting,

light tan plaid

Cutting Directions

From red, cut

4 triangles using template B

From black print, cut

1 - 3 1/8" squares

(or 2 triangles using template B)

From black and white shirting, cut

1 - 3 1/8" squares

(or 2 triangles using template B)

From light tan plaid, cut

1 piece using template A

To Make the Block

Draw a line from corner to corner on the diagonal on the reverse side of the 3 1/8" black and white shirting square. Place the square atop the black 3 1/8" square with right sides facing. Sew 1/4" on both sides of the drawn line. Use your rotary cutter and cut on the drawn line. Open the unit and press toward the darker fabric. This makes a half-square triangle unit. Each square will yield two half-square triangles. You need 2 for this block.

Follow the directions and construct the block on the diagonal.

Sew a red triangle on either side of the half-square triangle. Make two units like this.

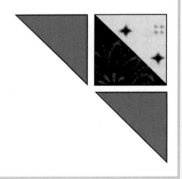

Sew the strips made from the triangles onto either side of the tan plaid strip to complete the block.

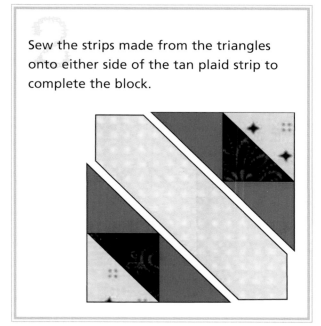

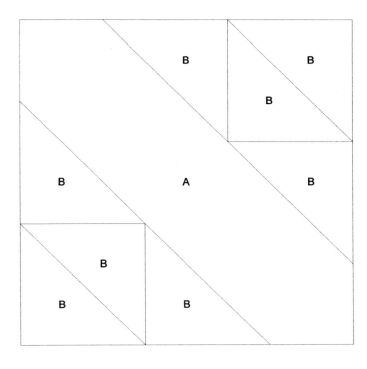

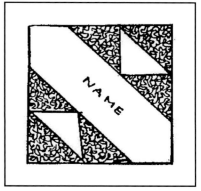

From **The Kansas City Star**,
April 5, 1944:
Number 742

A much desired quilt block pattern is the Friendship Name Chain, frequently used by organizations of women ambitious to make money. A small charge is made to each person desiring to have his or her name appear on a block. After the quilt has been completed further gain may be realized by selling it at auction. Mrs. Dollie Veatch, Route 2, Lancaster, Mo., is the contributor of the pattern.

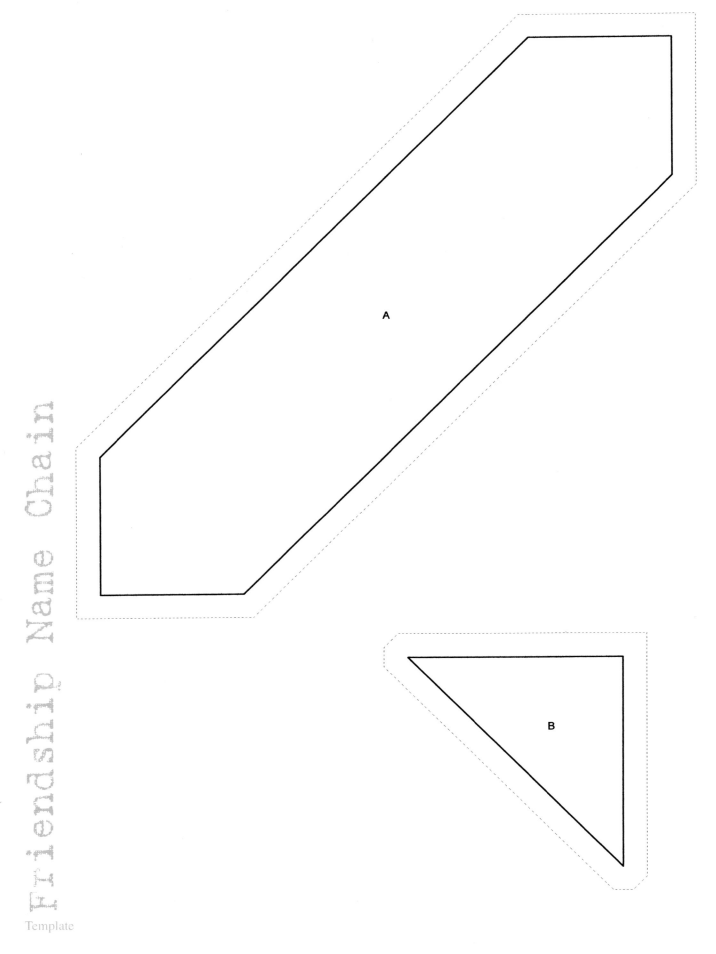

A

B

Template

Appeared in *The Star* **May 7, 1941**

Missouri Sunflower

Block Size: 12" finished

To Make the Block

Fold the 13" background square from corner to corner on the diagonals and lightly finger press the creases in place. Then fold the background square in half and in half again. Lightly finger press these creases in place. The creases will help with placement.

Sew the 12 petals together by sewing along the straight part of each petal until they form a ring. Stop stitching at the point where the petals begin to curve. Press the seam allowances under along the curved edges and pin the ring in place on the background fabric. Center the ring by matching the seams and the creases in the background fabric. Appliqué in place using your favorite method.

Fold the brown circle in half and in half again. Lightly finger press the creases in place. Line up the creases in the circle with the creases in the background fabric. Pin and appliqué the circle in place. After you have finished the appliqué work, press the block. Cut out the fabric that's behind the brown circle. Trim the block to 12 1/2".

Fabric needed:

1 - 13" square background fabric

Fat quarter of yellow

7" square brown for center

Cutting Directions

From the brown fabric, cut

one circle using template B

From the yellow fabric, cut

12 petals using template A

NOTE: The petals are not full enough to gather as they were in the original pattern.

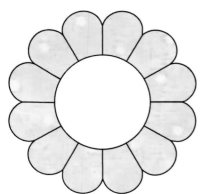

Missouri Sunflower

From *The Kansas City Star*,
May 7, 1941:
Number 647

The Missouri Sunflower design
is the creation of Mrs. William
Eagan, Flinthill, Mo. The center
is brown and the petals are
orange or yellow. Each completed flower is appliquéd on a
square of lettuce green. Mrs.
Eagan says each yellow petal
should be held a little full, or
gathered, as it is sewed to the
center.

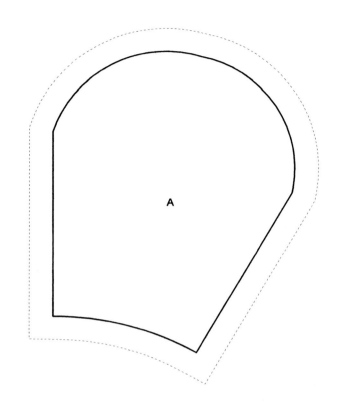

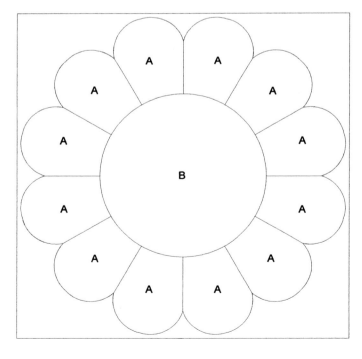

Missouri Sunflower

Template

B

Sapphire

Block size: 12" finished

Fabric needed:

light and assorted blues

Cutting Directions

From light fabric, cut

2 - 4 7/8" squares, cut once on

the diagonal or use template A

12 - 3 3/16" squares,

cut twice on the diagonal or use template B

From assorted blues, cut

1 - 4 1/2" square or use template C

12 - 3 1/4" squares,

cut twice on the diagonal or use template B

Sapphire

To Make the Block

Sew the B triangles together in rows as shown below.

Row one:

Row two:

Row three:

Row four:

Sew the rows together. You will need to make four sets of these.

Sew the rows to opposing sides of the center blue C square. Be careful that the triangles point in the correct direction.

Stitch the four angles closed. Begin sewing at the outer edge and sew toward the center square. Do not sew over the seam line of the center square, instead stop about three threads away. This way your seams and your block will lie flat.

Sew the A triangles onto the sides to complete the block. Press.

From The *Kansas City Star*,

September 2, 1953:

Number 929

A rich, blue sapphire is portrayed by piecing this block in blue and white. As sapphire is also known in green, purple and yellow, the quilt maker has opportunity to vary her color design. The pattern is a contribution by Mrs. Marie Johnson, Pegg route, Tahlequah, Ok.

History of the Block

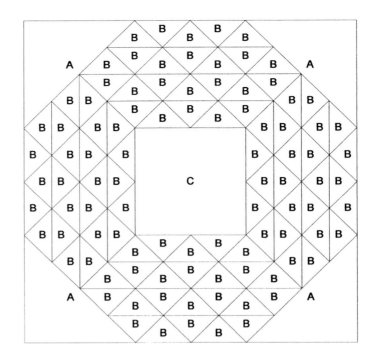

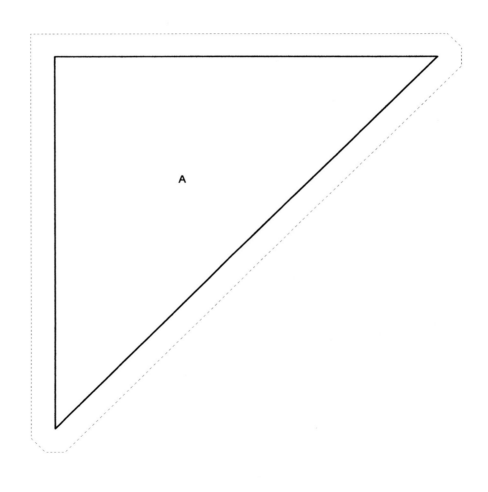

A

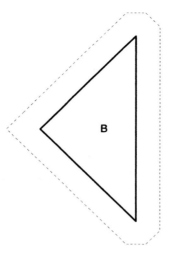

B

C

Template

Sunbonnet Sue

Block size: 10" finished

Appeared in *The Star* **August 9, 1930**

Fabric needed:

background, prints,

contrasting print,

green, white, skin-tone

Sunbonnet Sue

Finished Block Size: 10-inches square. Directions are for one block.

Make a template for each pattern piece using either freezer paper or template plastic. Do not add seam allowances to the templates. Place the pattern piece on the fabric and draw around the template. If you place the template on the reverse side of the fabric, Sue will face the opposite direction. Add 1/8-inch to 1/4-inch seam allowance when cutting each piece. Pin each piece in place and appliqué using your favorite method.

From background fabric, cut
1 - 11-inch square
(Trim to 10 1/2-inches after appliqué is complete)

From print, cut
1 - dress
1 - sleeve

From solid or contrasting print, cut
1 - bonnet
1 - shoe
1 - flower

From skin-tone fabric, cut
1 - arm

From green, cut
1 - small leaf
1 - large leaf

From white fabric, cut
1 - pantaloon

Embroider or embellish pantaloons, bonnet ribbon, flower stem and flower center to complete the block.

From *The Kansas City Star*,
August 9, 1930:
Number 109

Here comes "Sunbonnet Sue" to step demurely down upon your bed as a quilt patch and settle herself on a dressing scarf or form the motif for a quaint little boudoir pillow. Her dress may be either flowered or checked fabric and her cunning pantalettes a piece of embroidery or a ruffle of lace. Her bonnet, arm and foot can be of any harmonizing color, to be determined by the fabric chosen for the dress. The little figure is appliquéd on a block 9x11 inches and stripped together with bands of the solid fabric two inches wide. The flower may be used in each corner, which will be a 2-inch square of the same material as used for a background. Lay a piece of tissue paper over "Sue" and trace. Then cut out your patterns. A simple running stitch may be used after all edges have been turned in. This is a nice patch for little girls who are just learning to sew as it is comparatively simple, yet full of charm. Allow for seams.

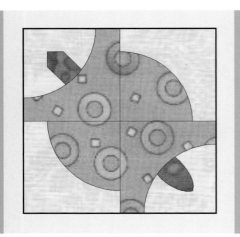

Turtle on a Quilt

Block size: 6" finished

To Make the Block

Fold the background A pieces in half and lightly crease the fold. Use the crease to position the head and the tail of the turtle. Appliqué the head and tail in place leaving the seam allowance that goes toward the body open.

Sew the background A pieces that have the head and tail appliquéd in place to the green B pieces. Make sure the head and tail both point toward the outside of the block.

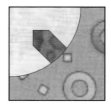 

Fabric needed:

light green print, dark green print and background

From the light green print, cut

2 pieces using template B

2 pieces using template A

From the background fabric, cut

2 pieces using template B

2 pieces using template A

From the dark green fabric, cut

1 head using template C

1 tail using template D

Turtle on a Quilt

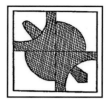

Sew the remaining green A pieces to the background B pieces. Then sew the four sections together as shown.

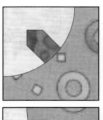

Turtle on a Quilt - Number 709
From *The Kansas City Star*,
January 6, 1943:

This is an instance where a turtle really put out his neck to supply a quilt block design. Mrs Addie Kennedy, Eagletown, Ok., is the contributor of the pattern.

Terrapin - Number 852
From *The Kansas City Star*,
April 13, 1949:

This favorite in her linen closet comes from Mrs. Lee Casey, Catalpa, Ark. (P.O., Ozone, Ark.). The head and tail of the terrapin are appliquéd. The other parts are pieced together. A small print is suggested for the turtle. The white pieces may be replaced by other 1-tone blocks, according to the pleasure of the quilt maker.

Turtle - Number 1043
From *The Kansas City Star*,
February 17, 1960:

Very appropriate as a coverlet for the bed of young son's room is the Turtle quilt, a design coming from Mrs. George Morris, Finley, Okla.

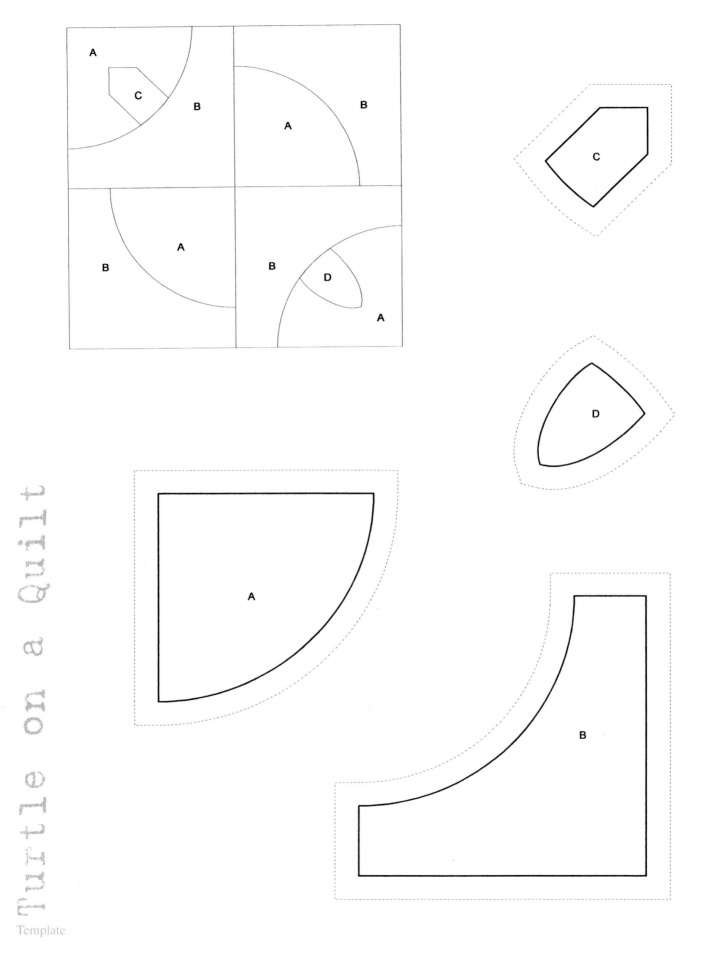

Turtle on a Quilt

Template

Turtle Time by Nancy Turtle. Quilted by Carol Faddis.

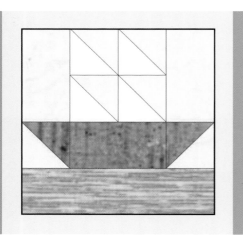

Sail Boat in Blue and White

Block size: 12" finished

This sail boat is made with white sails and a light blue background.

Fabric needed:

3 shades of blue - light, dark and medium

1 white

Cutting Directions

From medium blue, cut

1 - 12 1/2" x 3 1/2" strip.

This is piece C and no template is given

From dark blue, cut

1 - 3 7/8" square or

2 triangles using template B

1 - 6 1/2" x 3 1/2" strip or use template A

From light blue, cut

2 - 6 1/2" x 3 1/2" strips or

cut 2 pieces using template A

2 - 3 7/8" squares or

4 triangles using template B

From white, cut

2 - 3 7/8" or 4 triangles using template B

To Make the Block

(rotary cutting instructions)

Make 4 half-square triangle units using the light blue and white fabric and two half-square triangle units using the dark blue and the light blue fabric.

To make half-square triangles, draw a line from corner to corner on the diagonal on the reverse side of the lightest fabric. Place a light square atop a darker square and sew 1/4" on each side of the line. Use your rotary cutter and cut on the line. Open each unit and press toward the darkest fabric.

Sew the block together as shown.

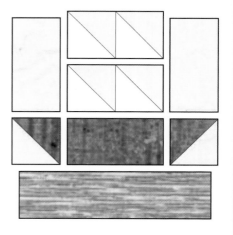

Sail Boat in Blue and White

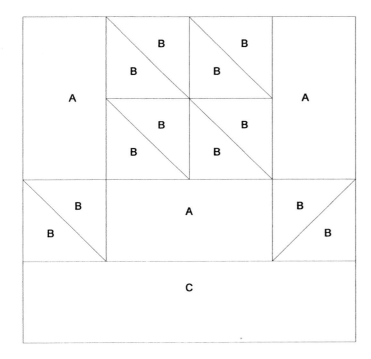

From ***The Kansas City Star***,
November 21, 1945:
Number 778

This sail boat design is one which was created by Mrs. Eli Roberts, Plattsburg, Mo., for a baby bed. It is just as pretty, she says, for a large bed.

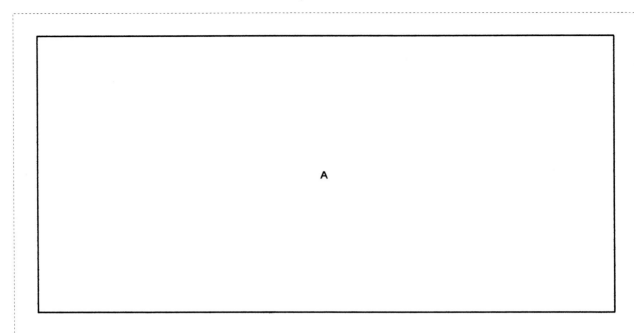

A

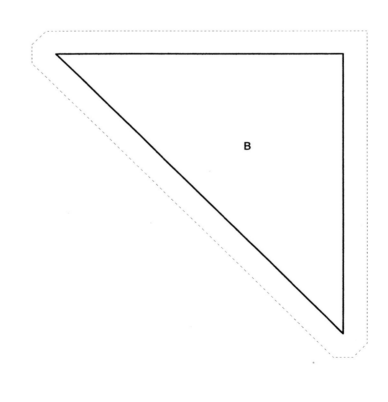

B

Sail Boat in Blue and White

Template

Appeared in *The Star* **November 9, 1938**

Block size: 12" finished

To Make the Block

Draw a line from corner to corner on the diagonal on the reverse side of the 4 7/8" tan squares. Place the tan square atop a dark green 4 7/8" square with right sides facing. Sew 1/4" on both sides of the drawn line. Use your rotary cutter and cut on the drawn line. Open the unit and press toward the darker fabric. This makes a half-square triangle unit. Each square will yield two half-square triangles. You need 8 for this block.

Sew three half-square triangles together as shown. Be careful that the color orientation matches the diagram. Make two rows like this.

Sew a half-square triangle unit to a tan square. Add a half-square triangle unit. This is the center row.

Fabric needed:

dark green and tan

From dark green, cut

4 - 4 7/8" squares

(or 8 triangles using template A)

From tan, cut

1 - 4 1/2" squares (template B)

4 - 4 7/8" squares

(or 8 triangles using template A)

Contrary Husband

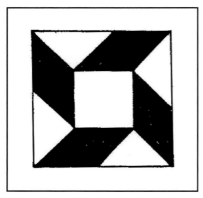

From *The Kansas City Star*,
November 9, 1938:
Number 564

The name of this pattern
"Contrary Husband," will
provoke conversation. It is an
attractive pattern in two colors.
This was sent by quilt fan, Mrs.
Cassie Rundel, Old Mines, Mo.
Thank you.

Sew the rows together as shown to complete the block.

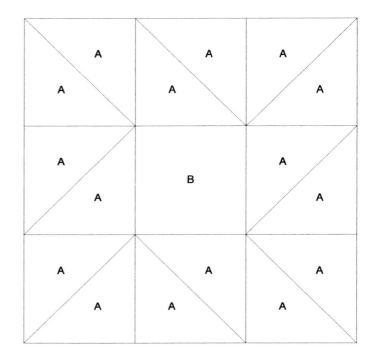

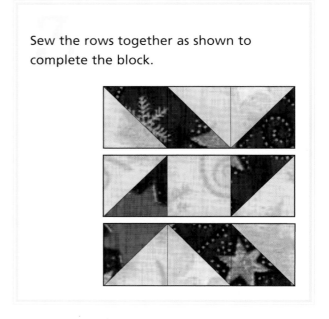

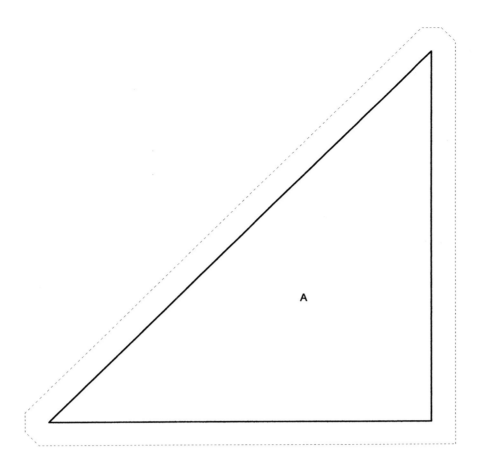

A

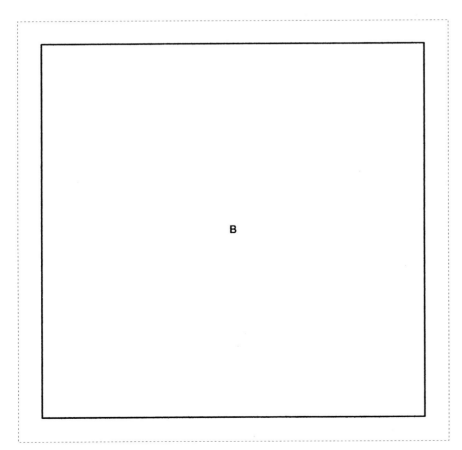

B

Template

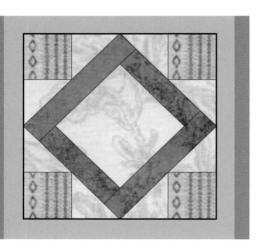

Friendship Quilt

Block size: 12" finished

Fabric needed:

Light tan or off-white

Rose

Rose and green print

Cutting Directions

From the light tan fabric, cut

1 - 6" square (No template given.)

4 - 3 7/8" squares - Cut each square once on the diagonal or cut 8 triangles using Template B

From the rose fabric, cut

2 rectangles using template C

2 rectangles using template D

If you would rather not use the templates for these two pieces, cut the two C rectangles 9" x 2" and the two D rectangles 6 x 2"

From the rose and green print, cut

4 - 3 1/2" squares (Template A)

To Make the Block

Sew a D rectangle to two sides of the 6 3/16" center square.

Now add the C rectangles to the other two sides of the square.

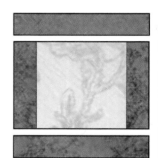

Make 4 corner units by sewing 2 B triangles to an A square as shown.

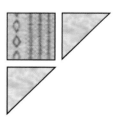

Sew the 4 corner units to the center square to complete the block.

From *The Kansas City Star*,
August 17, 1938:
Number 557

This is a pleasing form of the many album quilts sent by a loyal quilt fan to The Star. This leaves space for the name in pencil to be embroidered.

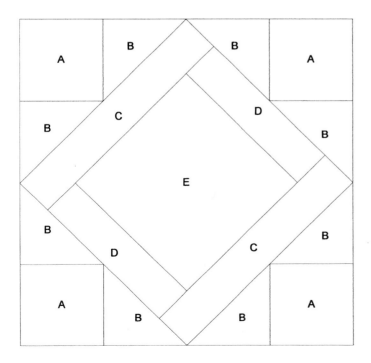

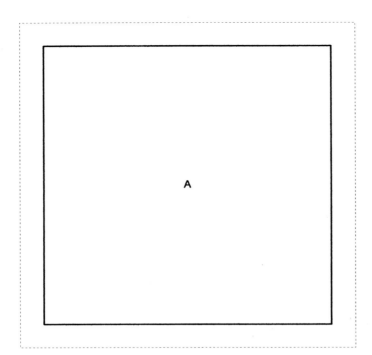

A

Friendship Quilt

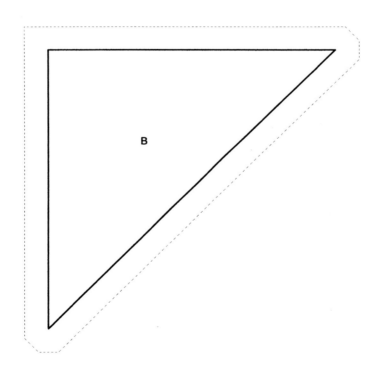

B

Template

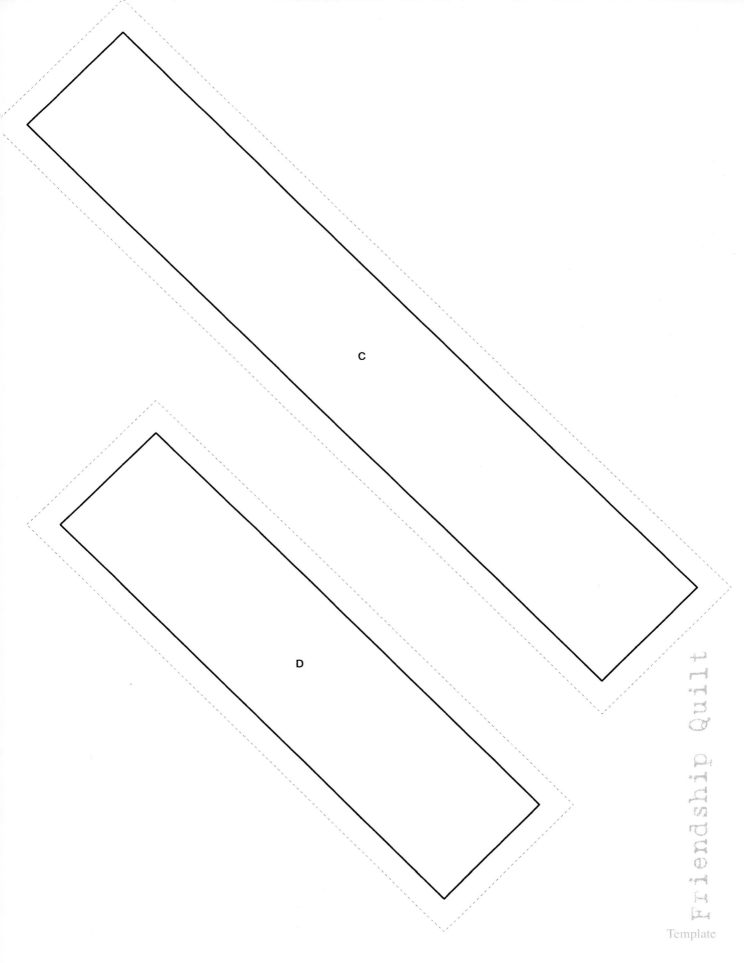

C

D

Friendship Quilt

Template

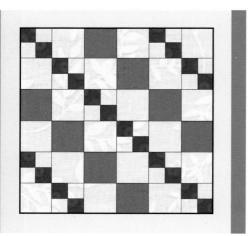

Carrie Nation

Block size: 12" finished

Sew the blue 1 1/2" strip to the background 1 1/2" strip. Press the seam toward the darkest strip. Cut the strip into 20 – 1 1/2" increments. Sew the pieces you have just cut into 4-patch units. You need to make 10 4-patch units.

To make the block, sew the pieces together into rows.

Row 1 (top) - Sew a four-patch unit to a background square. Add a red square, then another background square. Now sew on a 4-patch unit and end the row with a background square.

Row 2 - Sew a background square to a four-patch unit. Add a background square, then a red square followed by a background square. End the row with a 4-patch unit.

Row 3 - Sew a red square to a background square, then add a 4-patch unit. Now add a background square, then a red square and end the row with a background square.

Row 4 - Begin with a background square and add a red square and a background square. Follow this with a 4-patch unit, then sew on a background square and end the row with a red square.

Fabric needed:

red, cream and blue

Cutting Directions

From red fabric, cut

8 - 2 1/2" squares

From background fabric, cut

18 - 2 1/2" squares

1 - 1 1/2" strip across the width of the fabric

From blue fabric, cut

1 - 1 1/2" strip across the width of the fabric

Carrie Nation

Row 5 - Sew a four-patch unit to a background square. Add a red square, then another background square. Now sew on a 4-patch unit and end the row with a background square.

Row 6 (bottom row) - Sew a background square to a four-patch unit. Add a background square, then a red square followed by a background square. End the row with a 4-patch unit.

Sew the 6 rows together to complete the block.

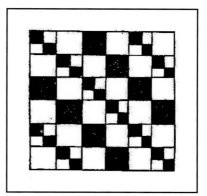

From ***The Kansas City Star*,**
December 4, 1940:
Number 632

The creator of this design, Mrs. V. Marshall of Medicine Lodge, Kas., has honored a famous prohibition campaigner with its title.

From ***The Kansas City Star*,**
November 12, 1947:
Number 814

One-tone color blocks for both sizes of squares create the most interesting impression in this design with conspicuous diagonal and vertical lines.

History of the Block

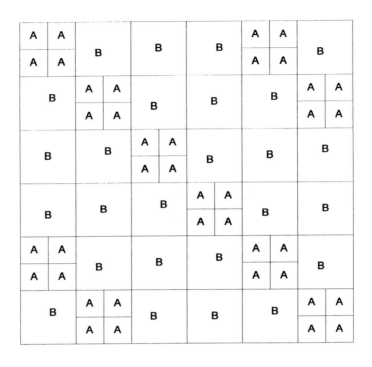

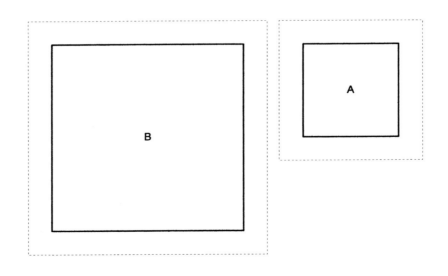

Template

Appeared in *The Star* **June 16, 1934**

To Make the Block

Draw a line from corner to corner on the diagonal on the reverse side of the 3 7/8" tan squares. Place the tan square atop a red 3 7/8" square with right sides facing. Sew 1/4" on both sides of the drawn line. Use your rotary cutter and cut on the drawn line. Open the unit and press toward the darker fabric. This makes a half-square triangle unit. Each square will yield two half-square triangles. You need 12 for this block.

Sew a tan 3 1/2" square to a red and tan half-square triangle. Now add a half-square triangle unit. End the row with a tan square. Make two rows like this.

Now sew 4 half-square triangles together as shown. Make two rows like this.

Crystal Star
Block size: 12" finished

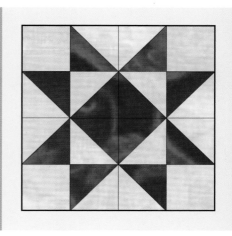

Fabric needed:
red and tan

Cutting Directions
From red, cut
6 - 3 7/8" squares
(or cut 12 triangles using template B)

From tan, cut
4 - 3 1/2" squares (template A)
6 - 3 7/8" squares
(or cut 12 triangles using template B)

Sew the rows together as shown to complete the block.

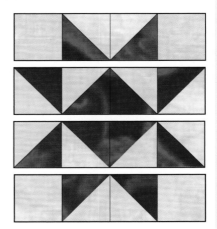

Crystal Star

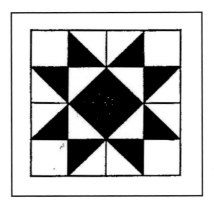

From *The Kansas City Star*,

June 16, 1934:

Number 358

This is a pattern that the most inexperienced quilt maker may use with confidence. Use any two colors desired. All seams are straight. Lemon yellow and green are good colors. Allow for seams. Next week a difficult quilt for expert quilters will appear.

From *The Kansas City Star*,

March 10, 1954:

Number 937

This is the Crystal Star quilt made by women of the Union Grove grange near Excello, Macon County, Missouri, which won first place in the 1953 Missouri grange quilt contest. It was presented recently to Mrs. Phil M. Donnelly, wife of the governor of Missouri. Mrs. Stanley Roebuck is home economics chairman of Union Grove grange. Other members of the grange are Mrs. Forrest Brock, Mrs. Marion Roebuck, Mrs. Gaylord Arnett, Mrs. Jesse Shannon, Mrs. Glen O'Toole, Miss Dollie Baker, Mrs. Annie Powell, Mrs. Arthur Richards and Mrs. Leslie Brock. The pattern was clipped from Weekly Star Farmer twenty years ago.

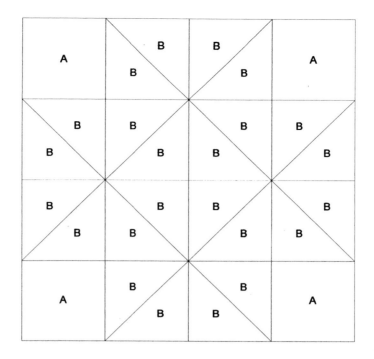

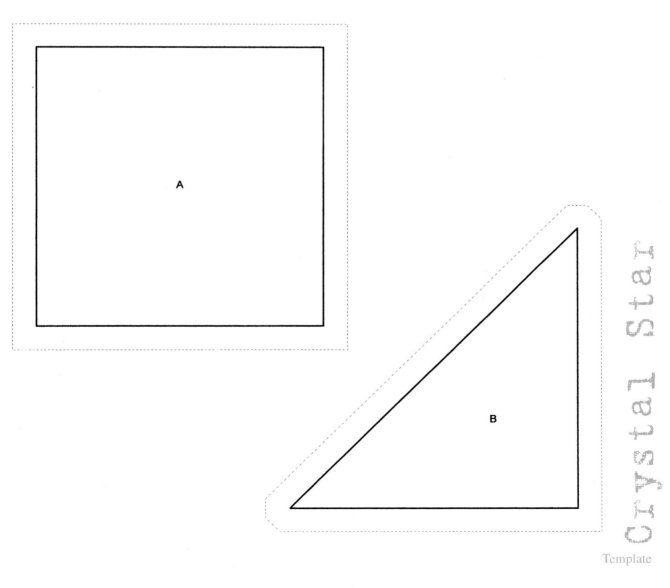

Template

Miz Sadie Turns 80 by Sandra Gilreath. Quilted by Pat Holston.

Appeared in *The Star* **August 6, 1930**

Goblet Quilt
Block size 6" finished

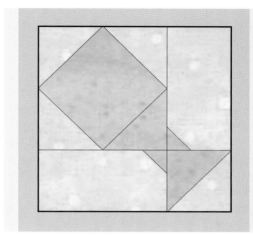

To Make the Block

Sew a D triangle to the A and C pieces.

Sew the background B triangles to the E square. Then add the contrasting B triangle.

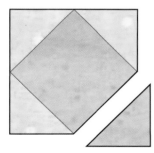

Sew the background B triangle to the contrasting B triangle.

Fabric needed:

Background and contrasting color

Cutting Directions

From background fabric, cut

1 piece using template A

1 piece using template C

4 triangles using template B

From contrasting fabric, cut

2 triangles using template B

1 square using template E

2 triangles using template D

Goblet Quilt

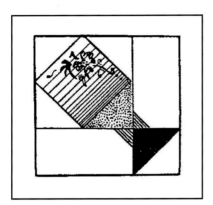

From *The Kansas City Star*,

September 6, 1930:

Number 113

The Goblet pattern may be developed in any solid color and white or pieced of a harmonizing color. A flowered piece for the large square and a very dark triangle for the base is suggested, as shown above. Striped fabric is pretty for the stem. This makes a small block only 5-1/4 inches square. Allow narrow seams.

Sew the block together as shown.

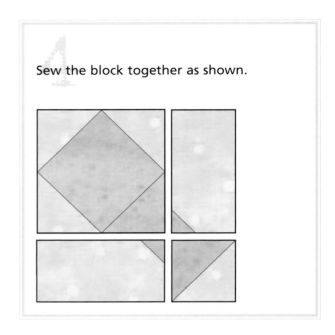

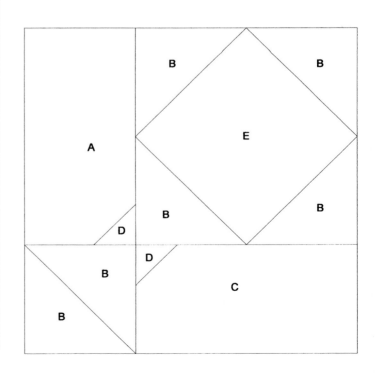

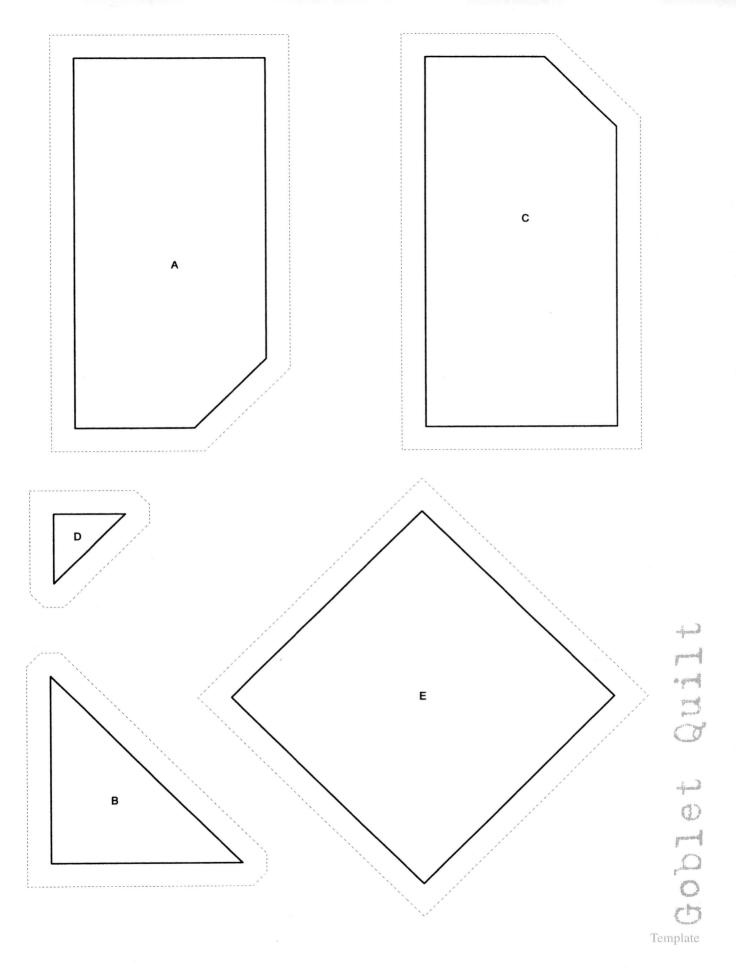

A

C

D

B

E

Goblet Quilt

Template

Pine Tree

Block size: 12" finished

Rotary cutting measurements for this block are not feasible due to oddly shaped pieces.

Fabric needed:
background, green and brown

Cutting Directions
From background fabric, cut
2 triangles using template A
1 each of template F, D, and E
3 squares using template C
36 triangles using template B

From green fabric, cut
42 triangles using template B
2 triangles using template G

From brown fabric, cut
2 triangles using template I
1 piece using template H

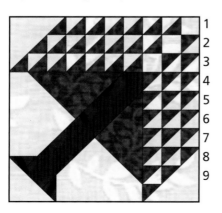

To Make the Block

Make half-square triangles by sewing a background B triangle to a green B triangle. Make 36 half-square triangles. Set these aside for the moment.

To make the lower part of the block, sew the brown I triangle to the background F piece. Add the green G triangle. Sew this to the brown H piece. Now sew the remaining brown I triangle to the background D piece. Add the remaining green G triangle. Sew this section to the opposing side of the tree trunk. Now sew the background E triangle to the base of the tree trunk.

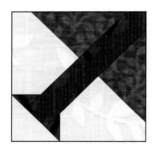

We are now ready to make the top of the tree. Always refer to the colored diagram for color placement orientation.

For row 1, begin with a green B triangle, add 6 half-square triangle units. Finish the row with a C square.

Pine Tree

Row 2, begin with a B triangle, and add half-square triangle units. Sew a C square and finish the row with a half-square triangle unit. NOTE: The last half-square triangle unit is turned in a different direction from the rest of the row.

Row 3, begin with a B triangle, add six half-square triangle units. Add a C square and finish the row with two half-square triangle units. NOTE: The last two half-square triangle units are turned in a different direction from the rest of the row.

Sew the three rows together and add a background A triangle. This is the top part of the tree. Set this aside for the moment.

Rows 4 - 7, sew 3 half-square triangles together. Check the color orientation.

Row 8, sew 2 half-square triangles together. End the row with a green B triangle.

Row 9, sew a half-square triangle to a green B triangle.

Sew rows 4-9 together. Refer to the colored diagram.

Add the remaining green B triangle to the bottom of the rows.

Sew a background A triangle to the three rows.

Sew this strip to the square you've made that has the tree trunk. Now add the strip made up of the first three rows to the top to finish the block.

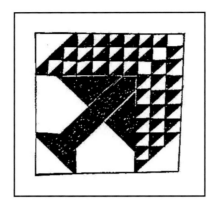

From *The Kansas City Star*, **September 19, 1928:**

Number 1

The pine tree blocks make a very handsome quilt. It takes sixteen pieced blocks to make a quilt about eighty-four inches square, aside from its border. These blocks must be set together diagonally with alternating blocks of white, cut the exact size of the pieced block. The above patterns are the exact size in which the pieces should be cut. The size of one block when put together is about fifteen inches. Seams must be allowed in addition, for quiltmakers differ in opinion as to seam width. The best way is to trace the patterns on cardboard, mark and cut to complete your pattern. Lay the cardboard patterns on the material. The pattern is drawn with pencil carefully. Cut a seam larger, sewing on the pencil line. The two white pieces of irregular shape have to be fitted in as marked on the edges; otherwise the "Pine Tree" is largely a business of sewing triangles into squares and adding them together.

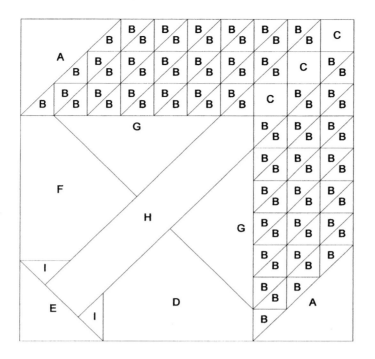

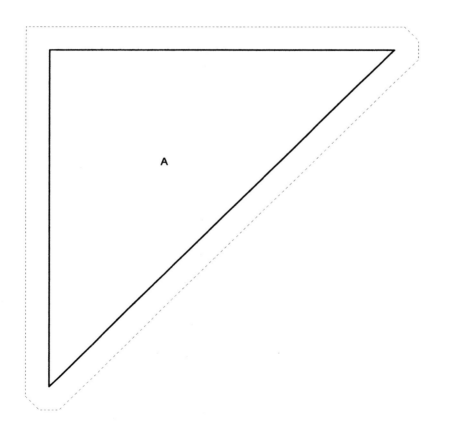

A

Pine Tree

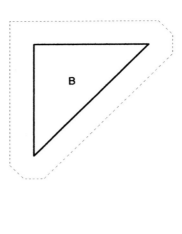

B

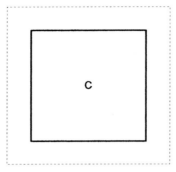

C

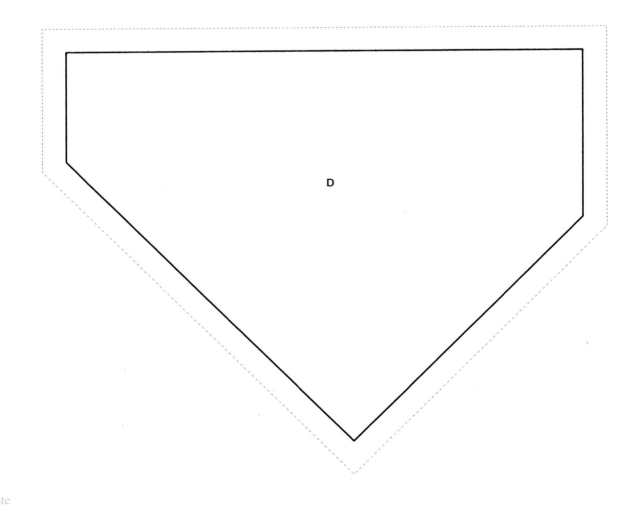

D

Pine Tree

Template

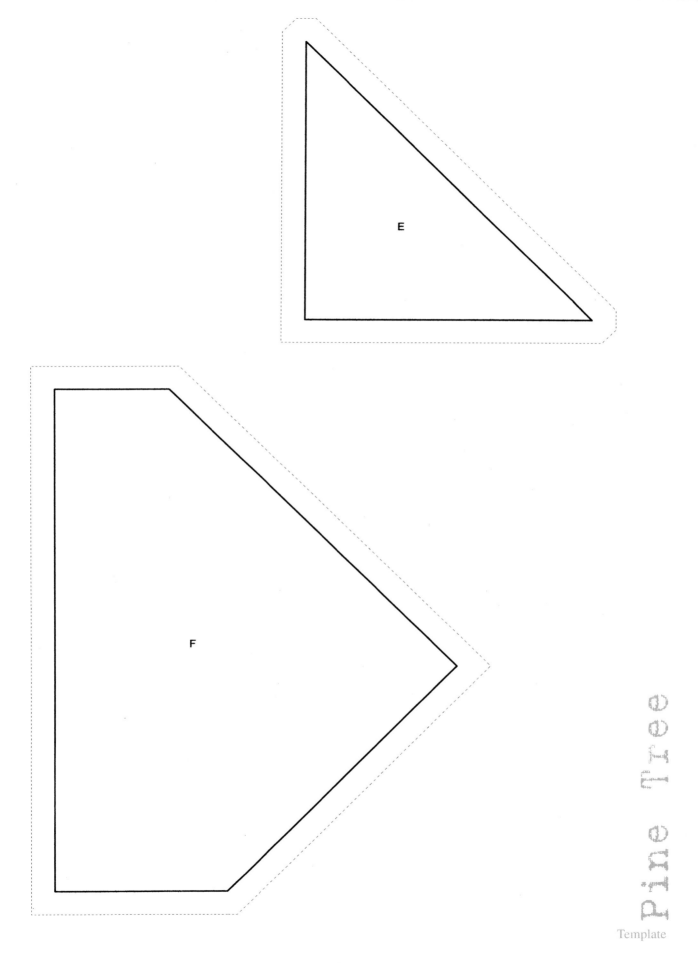

E

F

Pine Tree

Template

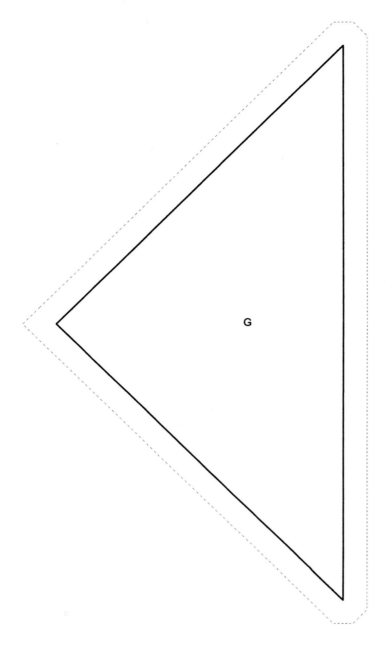

G

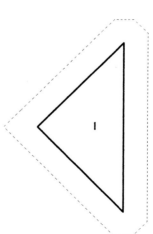

I

Pine Tree

Template

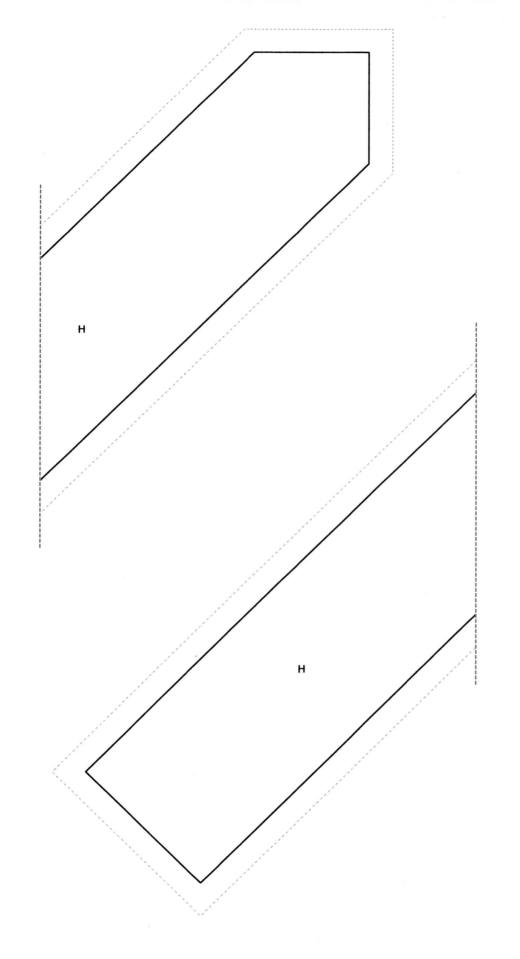

Join dotted lines to create template H

H

Join dotted lines to create template H

H

Pine Tree

Template

Saw Tooth

Block Size: 13" finished

Appeared in *The Star* **August 18, 1934**

Fabric needed:

dark, medium and background

Cutting Directions

From the dark fabric, cut

24 triangles using template F

1 - 1 1/2" square (template E)

From the medium fabric, cut

24 triangles using template F

4 - 1 1/2" x 6 1/2" rectangles (template D)

From the background fabric, cut

8 pieces using template A

8 pieces using template B

8 pieces using template C

To Make a Star Block

Make each of the six-pointed stars first. Sew a background A to a medium F triangle. Add a background C piece as shown.

Sew a background B piece to a dark F triangle. Add a background C piece as shown.

Sew five F triangles together. Begin with a dark triangle and alternated the colors as shown. Make another row of five F triangles. Begin this row with a medium triangle and alternate the colors.

Sew the two rows together and add a background B piece to each end as shown.

Saw Tooth

5 Sew the three rows together. Make four stars.

6 Sew a medium 1 1/2" x 6 1/2" strip to either side of the 1 1/2" dark square.

7 Now sew a star unit to either side of a medium 1 1/2" strip. Orient the stars so two dark points are pointing toward the strip. Make two of these units.

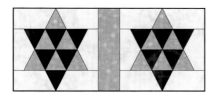

8 Complete the block by sewing the three rows together as shown.

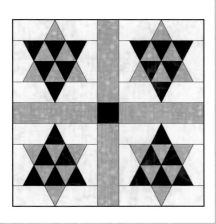

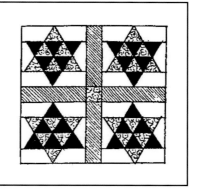

From *The Kansas City Star*,
August 18, 1934:
Number 367

An experienced quilt-maker contributed this pattern to The Star's quilt department. A sawtooth pattern of four stars. You can see at a glance that the colors selected will determine the beauty of the quilt. Allow for seams.

History of the Block

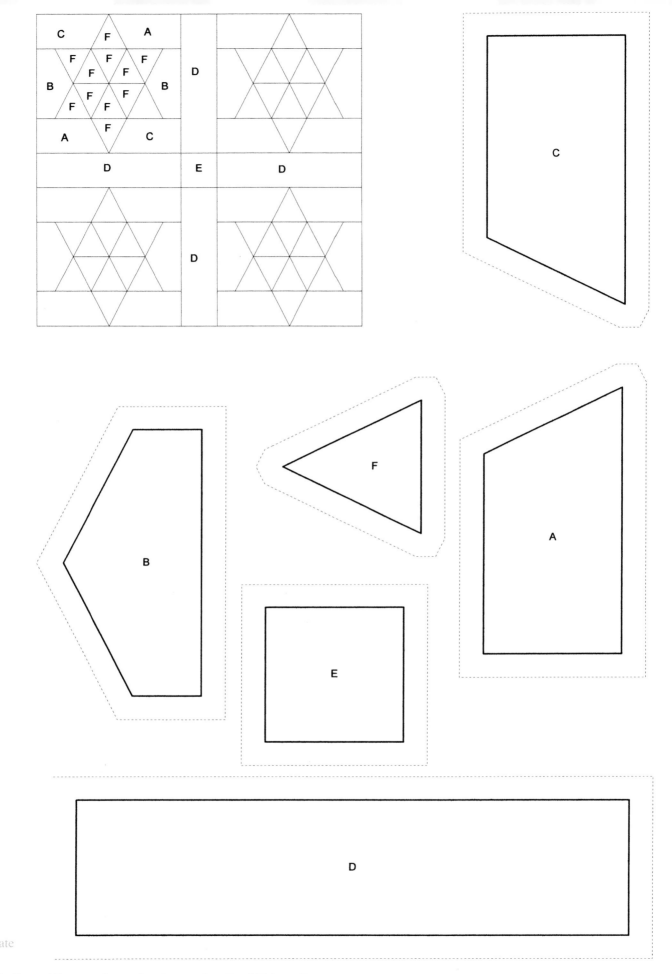

Appeared in *The Star* **September 5, 1945**

To Make the Block

Sew a red and black diamond together and add a B triangle. Make 4 of these units.

Now make 4 corner units by sewing a red and black diamond together. Inset the corner squares.

Sew the units into rows as shown. Add in the B triangles as you sew the units together.

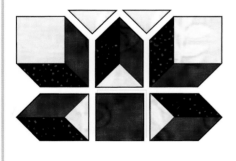

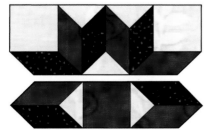

Quilt Mosaic

Block size: 12" finished

Fabric needed:

Light gray or off-white

Red

Black

Cutting Directions

From the light gray fabric, cut

4 - 3 1/2" squares (Template A)

3 - 4 1/4" squares

Cut each square twice

on the diagonal for 12 triangles

or cut 12 triangles using Template B

From the red fabric, cut

8 diamonds using Template C

1 - 3 1/2" square (Template A)

From the black fabric, cut

8 diamonds using Template D

Quilt Mosaic

From *The Kansas City Star*,

September 5, 1945:

Number 773

A visual effect of depth is created by choosing 1-tone colors for the rim and for the center triangles of this design, originated by Miss Lee Ellen Meyers, Star Route, Minco, Ok.

Sew the rows together. Inset the B triangles in the center row to complete the block.

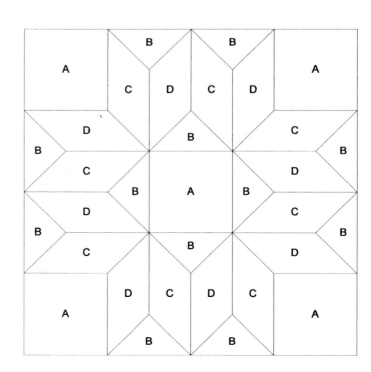

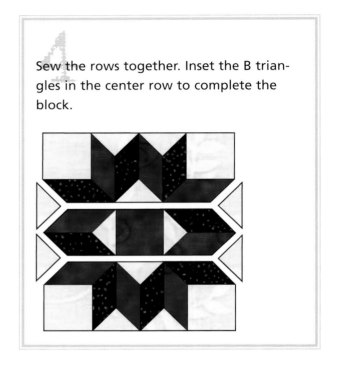

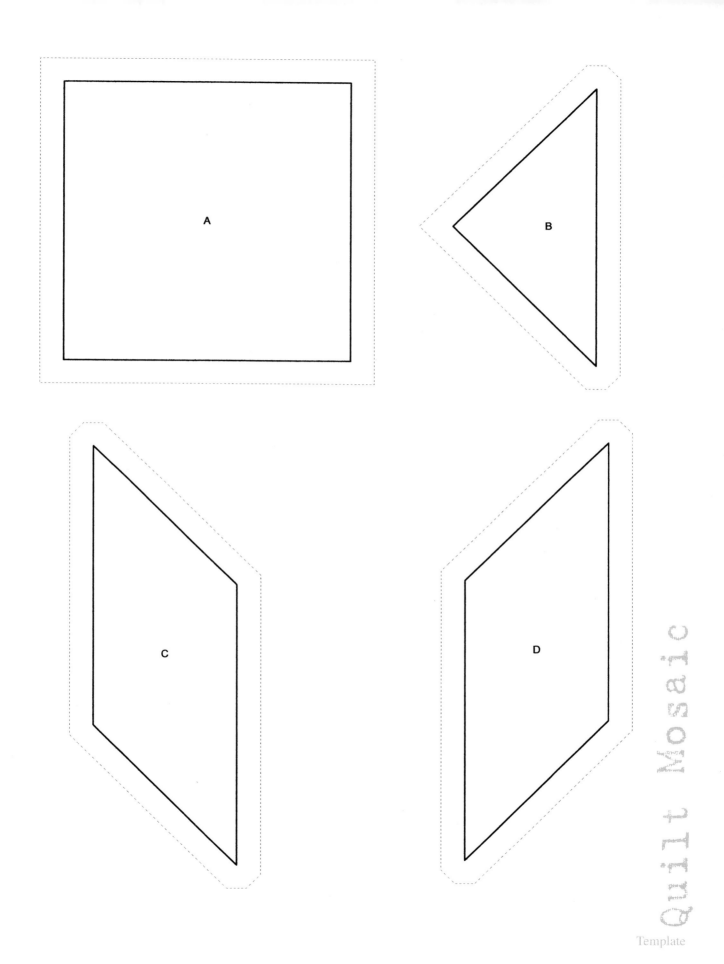

A

B

C

D

Quilt Mosaic

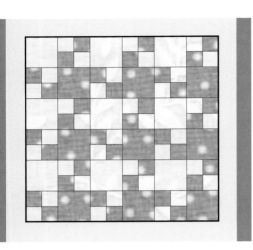

Cog Wheels

Block size: 12" finished

Fabric needed:

Blue

Cream

Cutting Directions

From the blue fabric, cut

9 - 2 1/2" squares (Template A)

36 - 1 1/2" squares (Template B)

From the cream fabric, cut

9 - 2 1/2" squares (Template A)

36 - 1 1/2" squares (Template B)

To Make the Block

Sew the blue and cream B squares together to make 4-patch units. Make 18.

Sew the four-patch units to the A squares in rows as shown. Sew the rows together to complete the block. Note the orientation of the four-patch units in each row.

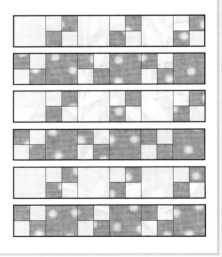

Cog Wheels

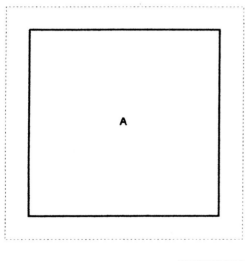

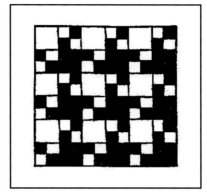

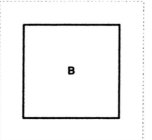

From ***The Kansas City Star***,
November 9, 1935:

Number 428

Cog Wheels is a quilt block that
Mrs. Mary K. Rogers,
Manhattan, Kas., designed to
use up the scraps that were left
after she finished a "Squirrel in
a Cage" quilt, the pattern printed in The Weekly Star last
week. The small scraps,
inevitable aftermath of any pattern quilt, may be conserved in
this design.

History of the Block

Cog Wheels

Template

Mary's Wheels designed and quilted by Suann Cole.

Appeared in *The Star* **August 12, 1933**

Economy

Block size: 12" finished

Fabric needed:

Light Tan

Medium Tan

Dark Brown

Dark Red

To Make the Block

Sew the A triangles to the E squares. You need 17 of these AE units.

Sew an AE unit to either side of a medium tan B rectangle. Make 8 of these strips.

Sew a B rectangle to either side of a dark brown D square. Make 4 strips like this .

To make the four corners of the block, sew the strips together as shown. Make four corner units.

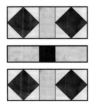

Cutting Directions

From the light tan, cut

34 - 1 7/8" squares.

Cut each square once from corner to corner on the diagonal, to make 68 triangles (Template A)

From the medium tan, cut

16 - 2 1/2" x 1 1/2" rectangles (Template B)

From the dark brown, cut

4 - 2 1/2" x 5 1/2" rectangles (Template C)

4 - 1 1/2" squares (Template D)

From the dark red, cut

17 - 1 15/16" squares (Template E)

(or cut 2" squares and use a

generous 1/4" seam allowance)

Economy

From *The Kansas City Star*,

August 12, 1933:

Number 318

After the other quilts are finished and the basket is full of scraps then is the time to start the "Economy" quilt. Colors will necessarily be hetergeneous but the block-effect of the quilt will give plenty of opportunity for variety.

Sew a corner unit to either side of a dark brown C rectangle. Make two strips like this.

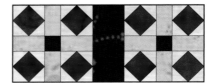

Sew a dark brown C rectangle to either side of an AE unit.

Sew the strips together as shown to complete the block.

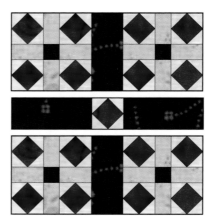

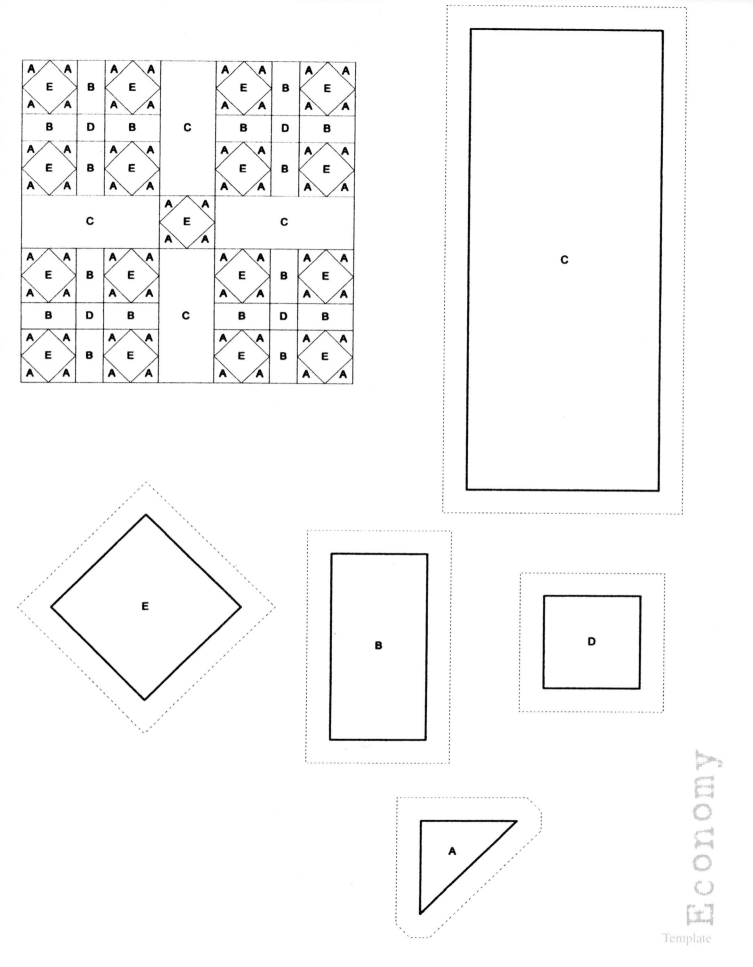

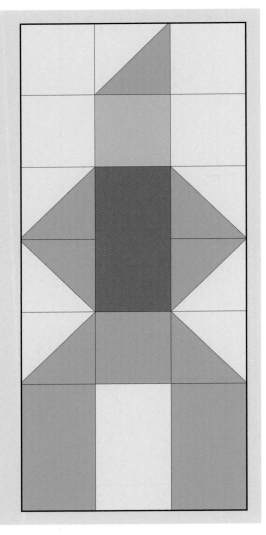

Soldier Boy

Block size 6" x 14" finished

This pattern was printed in 1944 and 1951. In 1957 it was printed again but used the name Soldier at the Window. In the first two printings, the pattern called for the soldier's torso to be made using two squares rather than a rectangle.

Fabric needed:

background, light khaki, dark khaki and skin tone

Cutting Directions

From background fabric, cut

4 - 2 1/2" squares (template A)

4 - 2 7/8" squares (or cut 7 triangles using template B)

1 - 4 1/2" x 2 1/2" rectangle (template C)

From skin-tone fabric, cut

1 - 2 1/2" square (template A)

From dark khaki, cut

1 - 4 1/2" x 2 1/2" rectangle (template C)

From khaki, cut

2 - 4 1/2" x 2 1/2" rectangles (template C)

1 - 2 1/2" square (template A)

4 - 2 7/8" squares (or cut 7 triangles using template B)

Soldier Boy

To Make the Block

Sew the patches together in rows beginning at the top.

Row 1: Sew a background square to a half-square triangle. Then add a background square to complete the first row.

Row 2: Sew a background square to a skin-tone square, then add another background square.

Row 3: Sew two half-square triangles together with the khaki triangles touching each other. Make 2 units like this and sew them to either side of the dark khaki rectangle.

Row 4: Sew a half-square triangle unit to either side of a khaki square.

Row 5: Sew a khaki rectangle to either side of the background rectangle.

Sew the rows together to complete the block.

From *The Kansas City Star,*
August 2, 1944:
Number 748

A fighting man in uniform is thus envisioned by Etta Hilderbrand, Beaver, Ok. White and khaki colored blocks construct the figure, while nose, eyes and mouth should be embroidered.

From *The Kansas City Star*,

June 6, 1951:

Number 893

Khaki and white are the only colors
required for this design. The mouth,
eyes and nose should be embroidered.

From *The Kansas City Star*,

July 10, 1957:

Number 1,009

Surprisingly easily is the "soldier"
picture window achieved. Mrs. Charlie
L. Catter, route 3, box 70, Apache,Okla.,
creator of the design, says the eyes, nose
and mouth should be embroidered.

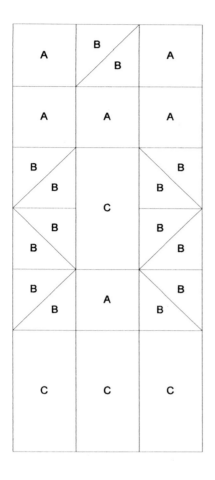

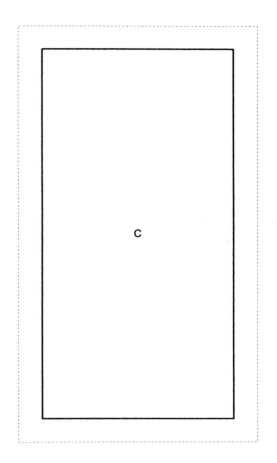

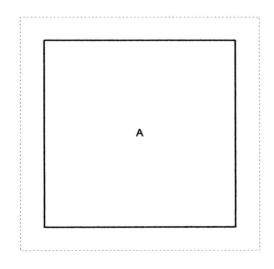

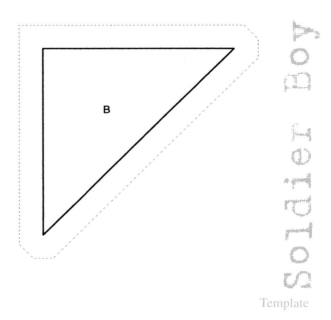

Soldier Boy

Template

Appeared in *The Star* **June 2, 1934**

Christmas Tree

Block size: 12" finished

Fabric needed:

dark brown,

dark green

and background

Cutting Directions

From background fabric, cut

1 - 6 7/8" square.

(2 triangles using template A)

3 - 2 1/2" squares

1 - 5 7/8" square

(2 triangles using template D)

Cut the square on the diagonal from

corner to corner.

6 - 2 7/8" squares

(12 triangles using template B)

From the dark brown fabric, cut

1 piece using template E

From the dark green fabric, cut

9 - 2 7/8" squares
(18 triangles using template B)
Cut 3 of the squares on the diagonal from
corner to corner. Reserve the remaining
squares for half-square triangles.

To Make the Block

For this block, you will need to make 12 half-square triangle units using the dark green fabric and the background. To make half-square triangle units, draw a line from corner to corner on the reverse side of the lightest fabric. Place a background square atop a dark green square and sew 1/4" on either side of the line. Use your rotary cutter and cut on the drawn line. Open each unit and press toward the darkest fabric.

We'll sew this block together in quarters.

Sew a dark green triangle to two half-square triangle units..

Sew a dark green triangle to a half-square triangle.

Sew the two rows together and add a dark green triangle to the top. Now sew the background A triangle to the rows as shown. Make two units like this, one for the upper left quadrant and one for the lower right quadrant.

Christmas Tree

4 Sew the remaining half-square triangle units and background squares together as shown. This makes the upper right quadrant of the block.

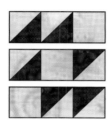

5 To make the lower left quadrant, sew a background D triangle to either side of the brown E piece.

6 Sew the four quadrants together as shown to complete the block.

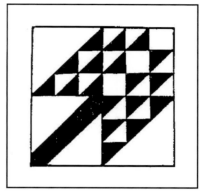

From *The Kansas City Star*,

June 2, 1934:

Number 356

A practical suggestion came to this department from a quilt fan. "Why not give us a pattern for a quilt that would make a suitable Christmas gift so we can be making it this summer and have it quilted in time for Christmas." Fine idea. Here is the answer - a green and white quilt in the pine tree pattern which will keep quilters busy all summer. Allow for seams.

History of the Block

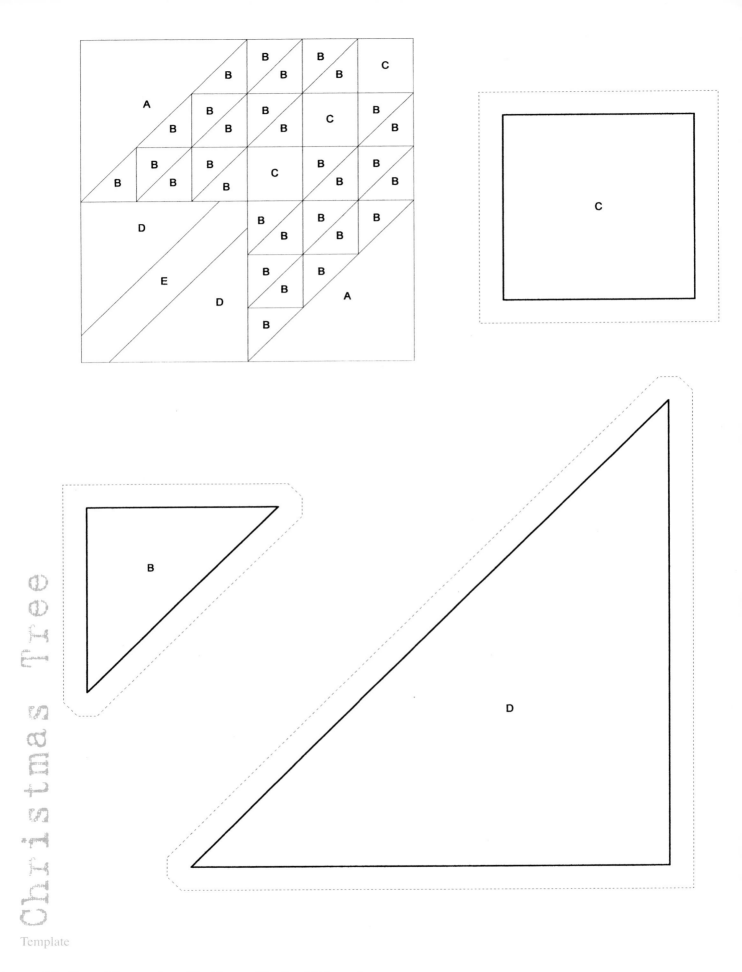

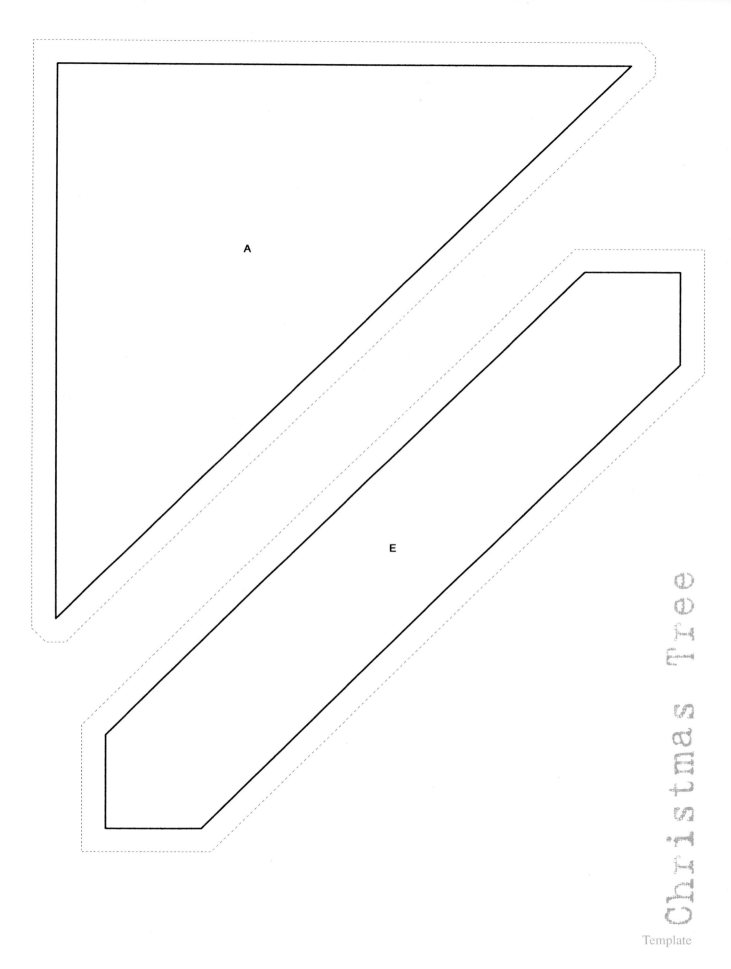

A

E

Christmas Tree

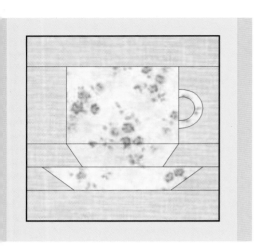

Coffee Cups

Block size: 6" finished

Fabric needed:

print and light green for background

Cutting Directions

From the print fabric, cut

1 - piece using template G

1 - piece using template I

1 - piece using template H

1 - piece using template J

From the green fabric, cut

2 - pieces using template A

2 - pieces using template B

1 - piece each using templates C, D, E, and F

To Make the Block

Stitch a B piece to the left side of piece G. Appliqué piece J onto the remaining B piece. Now sew the B piece with the cup handle appliquéd in place onto the right side of piece G.

Sew piece F to I, then end the strip with piece C.

Sew piece E to H, then end this strip with piece D.

Sew all the rows together as shown to complete the block.

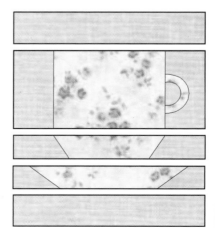

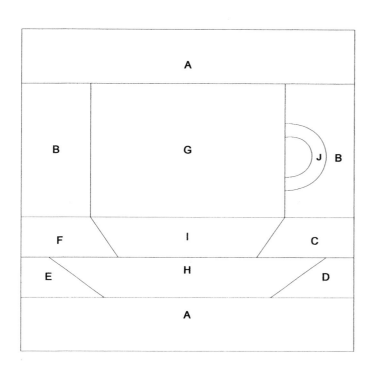

**From *The Kansas City Star*,
January 12, 1935:**
Number 385

The charm of a beautiful cup
appeals to all women. Here is a
design that can be made in
many attractive prints and plain
colors. Mrs. G. W. Schwarz,
Holton, Kas., contributed this
design to The Star. Thank you,
Mrs. Schwarz.

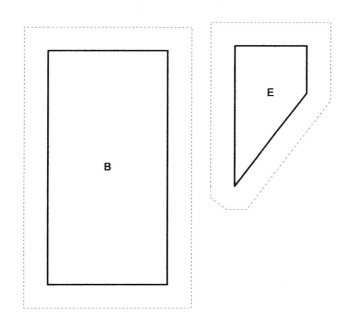

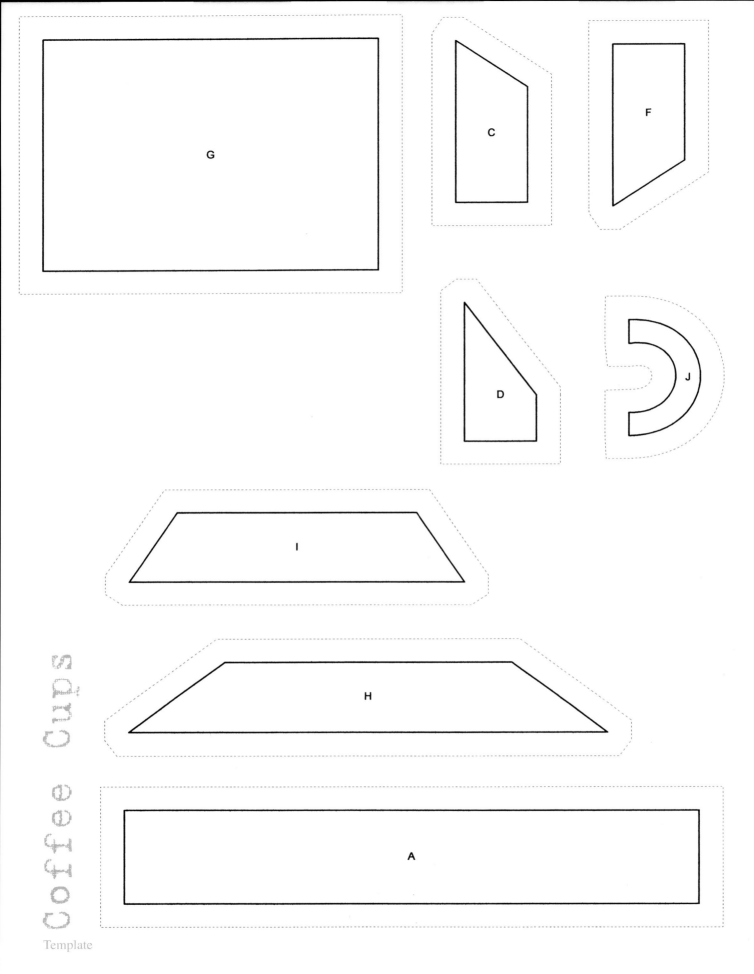

G

C

F

D

J

I

H

A

Coffee Cups

Appeared in *The Star* **June 13, 1936**

To Make the Block

Before you begin sewing, mark your seam lines. It is crucial that you do not sew beyond the quarter-inch seam line.

Sew a medium D piece to a dark F diamond, then add the medium E piece to the other side.

Pin, then sew the A piece to the diamond. Begin sewing at the top of the diamond and sew toward the E piece. Do not sew beyond the 1/4" seam allowance. Sew the seam between the A piece and the E piece closed. This will work best if you sew toward the diamond. Again, do not sew beyond the 1/4" seam allowance.

Add the C piece next using the same technique. Remove the piece from beneath the sewing machine foot. Start at the outside corner and sew the mitered seam in toward the diamond stopping before you sew into the 1/4" seam allowance. Make four of these corner units.

Turkey Tracks
Block size: 12" finished

Fabric needed:

dark, medium and light

Cutting Directions

From light fabric, cut:

4 pieces using template B

4 pieces using template A

4 pieces using template C

From medium fabric, cut:

4 pieces using template D

4 pieces using template E

From dark fabric, cut:

4 diamonds using template F

1 piece using template G

Turkey Tracks

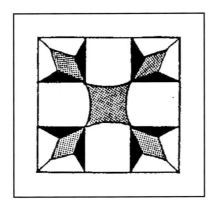

From ***The Kansas City Star*,**
June 13, 1936:
Number 459

This pattern was the inspiration for the quilt series in The Star. It was the first pattern offered in this series sketched from a quilt at The Star's Better Homes Show in 1928. There are many variations of the Turkey Track block and here is one that is pieced differently from the usual pattern. It was contributed by Ollie Wainwright, French, Ark.

Sew a corner unit to a B piece then add another corner unit. Make two rows like this.

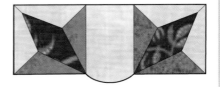

Sew a B piece to either side of the G piece. Make one row like this.

Sew the three rows together to complete the block.

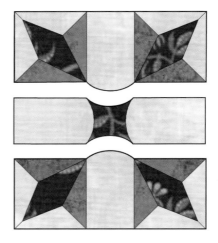

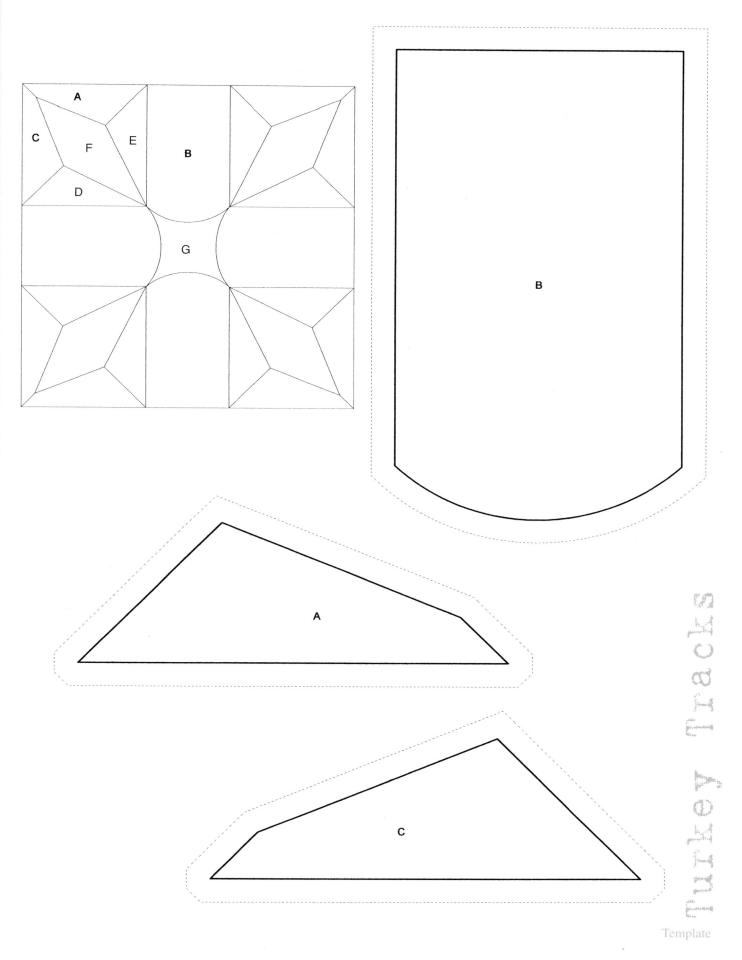

Template

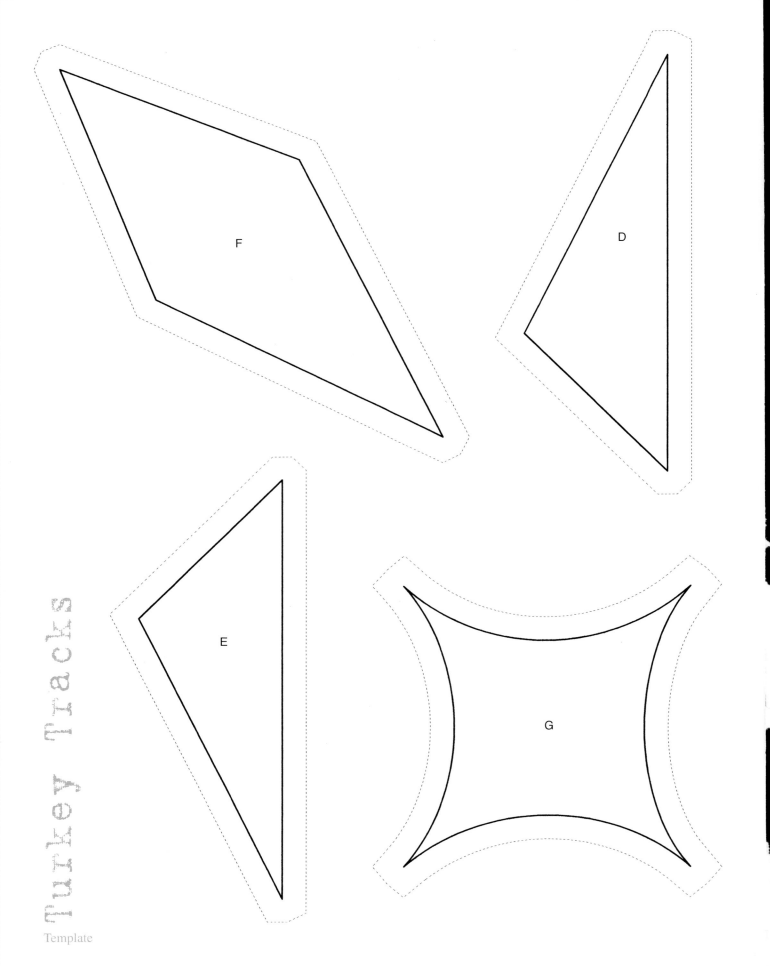

F

D

E

G

Turkey Tracks

Template

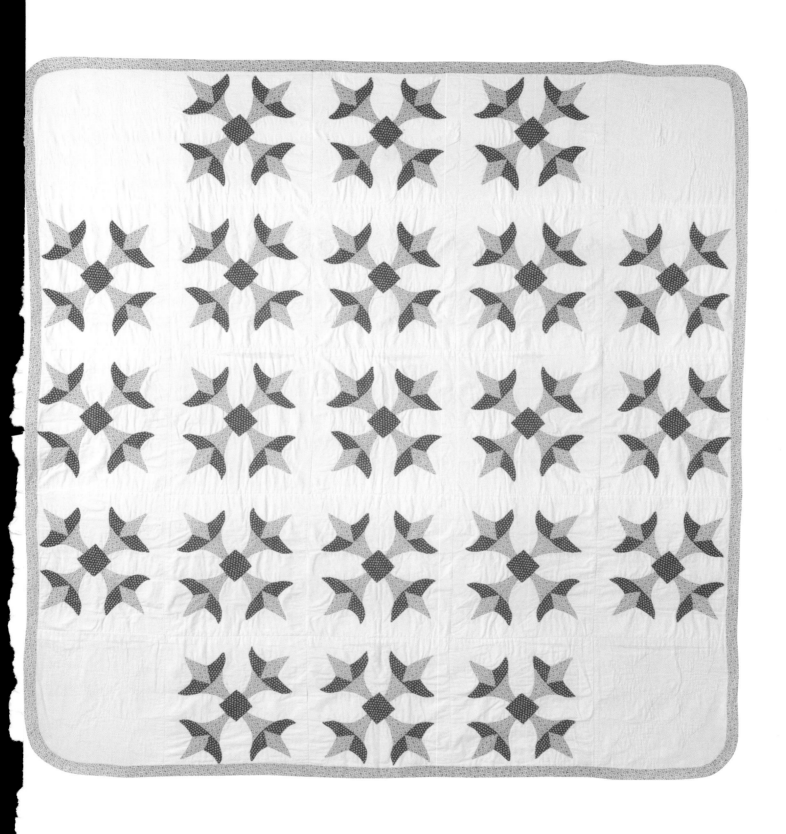

Turkey Tracks, owned by Wendy Dilllingham, quilted by Mayme Julia Jacobson Smith circa 1940 - 1950.